The
Fiction
Workshop
Companion

JON VOLKMER

is Associate Professor of English and Director of Creative Writing at Ursinus College in Collegeville, Pennsylvania. He holds an M.A. in Creative Writing from Denver University and a Ph.D. in English from the University of Nebraska, where he earned a Distinguished Teaching Award. A prize-winning fiction writer, he also has publications in poetry, writing theory, the personal essay, and travel and feature writing. Over a ten-year period, Dr. Volkmer has led dozens of workshops in large university, small college and non-traditional settings.

The Fiction Workshop Companion

Jon Volkmer

Director of Creative Writing

Ursinus College

BENDALL BOOKS
Educational Publishers

BENDALL BOOKS
Educational Publishers
CANADIAN ADDRESS: P.O. Box 115, Mill Bay, B.C. V0R 2P0
U.S. ADDRESS: 1574 Gulf Road, Unit 361, Point Roberts, WA 98281
ELECTRONIC MAIL: bendallbooks@islandnet.com
WORLD WIDE WEB: http://www.islandnet.com/bendallbooks

CATALOGING IN PUBLICATION DATA
Volkmer, Jon, 1956-
  The fiction workshop companion
  Includes index.
  ISBN 0-9696985-2-6
  1. Fiction—Technique. 2. Fiction—Authorship. I. Title.
PN3355.V64 1995   808.3   C95-910500-X

Printed in Canada
95 96 97 98 99 5 4 3 2 1

Contents

Stories are for joining the past to the future.
Stories are for those late hours in the night
when you can't remember how you got
from where you were to where you are.
Stories are for eternity, when memory is erased,
when there is nothing to remember except the story.

Tim O'Brien
The Things They Carried

This Book Is Your Friend

THIS BOOK starts from two assumptions that make it unlike other books for the fiction writing class. The first is that the textbook should be an accessory to the main business of the class, which is writing and workshopping stories. The second is that a fiction writing class can teach a lot of good things besides fiction writing.

Most teachers agree that writing stories and sharing stories is at the heart of fiction writing classes. That's why nearly every class is conducted as a workshop in which each student's work is discussed in turn by the teacher and classmates. And yet, books for writing classes seldom start with the idea of a student-centered classroom. Instead, the typical anthologies and textbooks are so hefty (and expensive!), so chock full of important writers and advice, that they seem to presume that all of the class time will be devoted to them.

This book proposes that you will learn more from each other than from Conrad and Chekhov. More from each other than from Updike and Morrison (Toni *or* Jim). I am not saying that you should not read. Of course you should. Read read read. On your own time and to your own tastes. And don't neglect the recommendations of teachers, writers, relatives and friends. Read everything.

But the writing workshop is something else. It offers a rare and precious commodity: a sympathetic captive audience. As much time as possible should be devoted to utilizing this commodity. For writers, the workshop is a laboratory where experiments in thought, style, and communication are carried out, and the results are obtained directly from the readers.

As in other laboratories, there is danger here. Readers may encroach on the writer's—and each other's—most cherished moral, aesthetic, and psychological beliefs. The mixtures can be volatile. The laboratory may blow up! So, as with other lab experiments, success depends on maintaining the proper controls. It is important to address the complex social and psychological dynamics of the workshop. Readers must not be jackals ripping the carcass of a story to shreds, nor must they waste each other's time blowing smoke. All of Chapter 4 is devoted to this topic, with useful protocols to help create the most effective writing workshop possible, and essential advice on being a good critic and on receiving criticism in the best way.

What makes a class a success? If we judge them only by those students who go on to have careers as writers, then nearly all classes are utter failures. But they are a big hit with students. It must be asked, therefore, what educational and human needs do these classes fulfill? What do students want from these classes? What can they get from them?

Chapter 1 addresses these questions. It places the writing workshop in its cultural and historical context, describes different kinds of enrichment fiction writing can bring, and presents a humanistic philosophy for the fiction workshop.

Chapter 2 orients you to the immediate task of writing a story. It shows you where to find your subject matter, tells you how to get started, and encourages you to get that first draft done.

Chapter 3 gets down to the nitty-gritty: the mechanical details, the techniques and strategies of effective fiction writing. At a basic level, story writing is a manufacturing job. This section gives you the tools to build a fine-tuned machine that will give readers a great ride.

If you have the tools, you still need the parts. Chapter 5, "The Parts Warehouse," uses an automobile supply store as a metaphor to govern a glossary of practical writing and literary terminology. More than a set of definitions, it is a lively concoction of clear explanations, goofy examples, and warnings about common mistakes. Don't worry, it makes sense if you're not a gear head.

The final chapter, "Stories," is just that. Just a few. None by Hawthorne or Dostoyevsky. None by any famous writers. These are touching, entertaining, contemporary stories that you could have written. In fact, all of these were written in fiction writing workshops, and all have been published. Each story is followed by a short discussion of how several fictional techniques are well employed.

This, then, is the *Fiction Workshop Companion*. Companion—as in friend, coach, helpful advisor. This book will save you time, inspire you, and head you off from common miscues which bedevil beginning writers. But it is not the central focus of your course. The main texts of a fiction workshop are the stories written and discussed by the workshoppers themselves.

A friend is not overbearing or intrusive. I have tried to design this book to be small, succinct, and inexpensive. I hope that it can be said to possess a true friend's diffidence; that is, it knows when to get out of the way.

To list all the writers, teachers, students, colleagues and friends who have made this book possible would take pages. My gratitude to all of you. Two major influences stand out: thanks to Tim O'Brien, whose fiction and thoughts on fiction have helped shape my philosophy; and to R.V. Cassill, whose *Writing Fiction* sets a high standard for a concise, personable textbook. Thanks, also, to Jay Connolly and Carol Dole for invaluable help in the preparation of this book.

Chapter One

Writing For Yourself

WHY ARE YOU taking a creative writing class? You're here, so you must have at least one answer to that question. Curiosity? A desire to express yourself? A school requirement? What you get out of writing will be in large part determined by what you expect to get out of it; therefore, it's logical for us to begin with a discussion of writerly expectations, motivations, and rewards.

What about money? Some people make a living writing fiction. A few become rich and famous. Why not you? Money and fame would be nice, but most of us are aware of what a long shot that is, and how much work is involved. Taking up writing for a shot at big money is like buying a lottery ticket that sentences you to twenty years of hard labor before you can scrape off the gum coating to see if you won anything.

Fortunately, there are many other rewards of fiction writing, rewards that range from making new friends to discovering truths about your own soul. In order to appreciate the possibilities, I think it's helpful to take a step back and locate the class in a cultural and historical framework. Then I will give you four very good justifications for the fiction writing workshop, and hope that these will assist you in the process of constructing your own expectations and motivations.

Creative writing, as a field of academic instruction, is a recent but wildly popular development in higher education. How the ball got rolling is anyone's guess—a dozen universities claim to have invented the graduate writing degree as far back as the 1930s. David Fenza at Associated Writing Programs sees a connection between the early popularity of writing workshops and the post-World War II influx of G.I.'s into the universities. "They all had stories to tell," he says, "war stories."

However it began, the seeds of writing spread on the wind and took root. Besides all the graduate writing programs, nearly all undergraduate English programs in the country have course offerings in creative writing, and it's now common in high schools as well. Most colleges and universities have at least one in-house poet or fiction writer, often several of each. By the mid-1990s, Associated Writing Programs had 279 affiliated programs, and Fenza estimates the number of students taking creative writing courses to be in the tens of thousands.

The writing craze has not been confined to the academy. Informal writing workshops flourish in libraries, church basements, prisons, and living rooms. Across North America, the writing group has replaced the reading group as the preferred social hobby of literary types.

Some people are not happy about this trend. The most extreme doomsayers will suggest that we have gone from a nation of good readers to a nation of bad writers. That it reflects our national egoism and self-obsession, the loss of standards, and the decline of Western Civilization.

My outlook is brighter. I see the popularity of creative writing as simply another aspect of a massive decentralization and democratization in our society. Look around: in an eyeblink, we've gone from a handful of look-alike television networks to hundreds of channels, with community access to give Jane Citizen her fifteen minutes of air time, if not fame. We've gone from Budweiser's overwhelming market share to regional micro-breweries to batches of home brew in our basements. From Frank Sinatra to thousands of bar bands doing "New York, New York" to me belting it out to the Karaoke machine. Everywhere, the trend is to greater audience segmentation, more participation.

The point is not that I sing better than Frank Sinatra (I don't) or that my home brew is better than Budweiser (it is), but that my life is more enriched by enacting than by witnessing. Nike's advertising agency captured the spirit of the age when it coined the ingenious three-word slogan: "Just do it."

Which brings us back to the reasons that you, in particular, are taking a creative writing class, and the kinds of benefits you might expect to find there. The critic William Empson once proclaimed unambiguously that there are seven types of ambiguity, and proceeded to describe each one. I will risk opening myself to seven types of ridicule by outlining the four types of enrichment that the writing workshop can provide.

1. Financial Enrichment: The Beautiful Dream

"No man but a blockhead ever wrote, except for money."
— *Samuel Johnson*

People will pay you a lot of money for your stories. Well, no, actually, they probably won't. Aside from a handful of marquee names, not many fiction writers are making money in fiction these days. Even many well-established and critically applauded novelists have difficulty finding a readership.

For short story writers, competition is stiff. Prominent magazines such as *The New Yorker* and *The Atlantic Monthly* get thousands of submissions every year, and accept very few from writers who are not already well known. There is more opportunity with the hundreds of literary reviews—everything from *Antioch Review* to *ZZYZZYVA*. These magazines, often called "quarterlies" after the usual frequency of publication, carry varying amounts of prestige, but most have small readerships and offer negligible compensation. The most common form of payment is two free copies of the issue in which your story appears. Even so, their editors are inundated with manuscripts, many of them from professional writers. It's been noted that if everyone who writes fiction would just buy a couple of novels a year, and subscribe to one literary magazine, the publishing world would be a whole lot more robust.

You could be one of the fiction writers who gains recognition and makes money. We all have the dream, and there is nothing ignoble in trying. Fate can be strange. If *The Bridges of Madison County* can be a best seller, truly anything is possible.

On the other hand, if you adopt Sam Johnson's motto, you set yourself up for disappointment and frustration. Trust me, you are not a blockhead just because your writing doesn't make money. Other forms of enrichment are attainable. I would like to make the case for three splendid ones.

2. Intellectual Enrichment: Mastery of a Discipline

True Ease in writing comes from Art, not Chance,
As those move easiest who have learn'd to dance.
  — Alexander Pope

There is something intrinsically beautiful in the study of an intricate discipline. As with other forms of art, fiction writing is sleight of hand—a large part of its beauty is its seeming effortlessness. At the ballet, we do not see the dancers sweat or feel their knee ligaments strain; we marvel at their gravity-defying lightness. At the jazz club, we don't have to sit through the endless practice sessions that blessed the pianist with the ability to improvise.

So it is with writing. We are most enraptured when the story spins out seamlessly, effortlessly, breathlessly, as if it could not possibly have come out any other way. The writer takes pains to mask the clunking fits and starts of the creative process. As Yeats put it,

A line will take us hours maybe;
Yet if it does not seem a moment's thought,
Our stitching and unstitching has been nought.

A short story is a Frankensteinian enterprise, or—to invoke cinematic terminology—a morphing job. Your product must have the look and feel of real life, must be utterly convincing in its simulation. And yet it is artificial, a construct. And, from a parts-supply-warehouse perspective, your materials are limited. Part of the joy of writing comes in wandering the warehouse, learning the names of the whizmoes available to you, and examining how other morphers have used them.

It is possible, of course, to make this voyage of discovery inductively, intuitively, without formal instruction. Many writers have done it that way. Others have toured the museum of literature in the company of learned professors who point out the nuances of technique by which the masterpieces were accomplished.

But I prefer the "Just Do It" approach, Parts Warehouse instead of museum, and that's where the fiction workshop and this little book can help.

A tinkerer in pocket watches may never build a working watch. A ballet student may never perform on stage. An oenophile may never bottle her own wine. And yet, in each case, there is exquisite pleasure in the learning. When one has an understanding of the constituent parts—mainsprocket, *pas de deux*, fermentation—one's appreciation of the process and product is immeasurably enhanced. You may never write the perfect short story, but you will greatly add to your ability to see glimpses of perfection in others. And that in itself is great reward.

3. Social Enrichment: Fascinating Intercourse

"O, I never said such a thing!"
"O, but you did!"
"O, but I didn't!"
"Didn't she say that?"
"Yes. I heard her."
"O, there's a . . . fib!"
  — James Joyce

Did I say *intercourse?* It's such an unwieldy word when applied to sex, yet so graceful in its infrequent other applications. Writing fiction is very much a matter of the heart—you have to feel it to write it. And yet, as the previous section indicates, it's also inescapably an intellectual discipline. In the workshop, both your heart and your mind will be on display. Consider the many and complex roles you will play in the fiction workshop. To others you will be friend, cheerleader, devil's advocate, critic, and coach. When your own work is on the table you will be like a proud but anxious parent, with multiple layers of identification for characters and situations you have created. The end result is one of the most complicated, fascinating and intense social situations you are ever likely to encounter, an inter-coursing of interpersonal interchange.

It will sometimes be tense; it can be explosive. I have, with my own eyes, witnessed two burly poets shoving each other in the chest, saying, "Oh yeah? Well your synecdoche sucks. You wanna take this outside?" I have seen people cry.

The fiction workshop, as social interactive space, must be carefully set up, and to some extent managed, to make full use of its dramatic power, to get to the heart of story-writing, and to safeguard participants from needless harm. More on this in Chapter Four.

4. Metaphysical Enrichment: Creation of Personal Mythologies

I'm skimming across the surface of my own history, moving fast, riding the melt beneath the blades, doing loops and spins, and when I take a high leap into the dark and come down thirty years later, I realize it is as Tim trying to save Timmy's life with a story.
— *Tim O'Brien*

Here, saved for last, is what I consider to be the most powerful argument why you should take the fiction writing class, why everyone should be writing fiction: we can create personal mythologies that make sense of our lives. Most of us lead our lives without much reflection. The days reel off, become months and years, and we never have time to make sense of anything. Our beginnings, middles, and ends are determined by things outside of us: alarm clocks and semester breaks, appointment books and anniversaries. When crises occur, when climaxes happen, we're too caught up in the drama of the moment to reckon what it means in the overall context of our lives.

One classical definition of art is that it imposes order on chaos. It interprets and gives meaning to that which is formless. In the unravelling, formless movie of our lives, it can be an act of self-revelation, even self-construction, to go back and snip out a section, edit it for this effect and that, make up new sequences, and come up with a finished film that isn't exactly what happened, but has more truth than what did.

Can writing fiction discover more profound truth than diary, memoir, autobiography? In answering yes, I'm taking sides in an argument that goes back at least as far as ancient Greece. In creating his utopia, Plato, you will recall, tossed the poets out on their backsides. Why? They lie. History is already one-step removed from Truth. Poetry, being a doctored version of history, distances us farther.

But Aristotle didn't cotton to the dreary chained-up-in-a-cave version of reality, and in *The Poetics* he took the opposite tack, avowing, "Poetry, therefore, is a more philosophical and a higher thing than history: for poetry tends to express the universal, history the particular."

And Plato, as any good historian will tell you, was wrong. There is no such thing as History, only various versions of history. The diary entry about robbing the liquor store today will be a wholly different account than the one you write next week in prison. Sorry, Joe Friday, there's no such thing as, "Just the facts, Ma'am."

In *The End of the Road*, John Barth has a fictional narrator who makes precisely this point with gusto:

> Articulation! There, by Joe, was *my* absolute, if I could be said to have one. . . . To turn experience into speech—that is, to classify, to categorize, to conceptualize, to grammarize, to syntactify it—is always a betrayal of experience, a falsification of it; but only so betrayed can it be dealt with at all, and only in so dealing with it did I ever feel a man, alive and kicking. . . . When my mythoplastic razors were sharply honed, it was unparalleled sport to lay about with them, to have at reality.

Great sport, yes, but also great truth. Aristotle and I are telling you that fiction writing is a way to make meaning out of your life, or parts of your life. By lying about the mere historical details, you seek to achieve a higher universal truth on a plain that makes sense to you and to your readers, and helps you own your past in a more meaningful way.

Let me share a personal example. For five summers that encompassed my adolescence, I worked in my father's grain elevator in rural Nebraska. It was hot, dirty, dangerous work. My father was a stern taskmaster. I was pretty much miserable. A few years later, as a college sophomore in my first writing workshop, I was casting about for a subject on which I had strong feelings and vivid experiences. I turned back to my days as an elevator man.

For my early drafts, I let the external world determine the parameters of my story. That is, I thought it should begin at the end of the school year, when I started my annual job, proceed through the Fourth of July winter wheat harvest, include the late summer emptying of the elevator in preparation for the main harvest in fall and build to the fall harvest of corn, milo, and soybeans, when farmers' trucks full of grain were lined half-way up Main Street, the elevator was open twenty hours a day, and the countryside went into a collaborative frenzy to get the harvest out of the fields before the weather turned wet. It was an annual rising action and climax, natural as the seasons, just waiting for me to transform it into art.

I worked on that story for ten years, ground out twenty or thirty versions, and shepherded some of them through fiction workshops. The chronology of the story grew shorter and shorter as the rhythms of my life and concerns gradually subsumed the external rhythms of the seasons, until, in the version published by *Prairie Schooner* in 1986, the action of the story occurs over the space of six hours of one day in August, and concerns the emptying of one bin of grain. My job, as short story writer and personal mythologist, was to compress five summers of experience into six emblematic hours.

And still, I wasn't done. I couldn't leave that story alone. I rewrote it again and again, and discovered, through writing, that I had been ignoring or suppressing a key piece of the puzzle. It was during my time as an elevator man that my mother died of cancer, and I realized that I would never get at my real truth until and unless I acknowledged that awful reality within the story.

So I worked another five years. Finally, I believe that I can let it go. The point is, in actual fact-by-fact detail, dialogue, and event, the current story is farther from accurate history than it has ever been. I never lived the day described in the story. And yet I lived or imagined each moment that occurs in the story. The facts of the story may be lies, but the mythopoetic entirety of the story is the purest Truth I have ever found.

THE ELEVATOR MAN

by Jon Volkmer

Some said it was corn killed a man first. Tim's dad said it had something to do with that particular smell of corn. Like coughing up lungfuls of Green Giant creamed style, he said. Wilmer figured beans was the worst. You don't get your big clouds of dust with soy beans, he'd say, but there was something kind of oily the way it stuck to your throat and lungs. Wheat was bad. Everybody knew wheat was bad, but around southern Otoe county it was mostly hard red winter wheat, and when you're harvesting around 4th of July you're too hot to worry much about dust.

Tim knew milo was worst of all. He was only twelve, but he had Vaughn Jones to back him up. Vaughn had operated the grain elevator over in Talmadge for fifty-one years before he retired and moved to Julian. Tim saw him shuffle past every day on his way to get his mail at the store, pulling that oxygen bottle on little wheels behind him. When Vaughn Jones pointed to the cloud of red dust rising up out of the back end of the truck when the milo was pouring in, shook his head and said that was the most killing grain dust there was, you had to believe it. Vaughn said milo didn't have civilized uses like your corn, wheat, and beans, making bread and like that. Milo was just your basic hog feed.

They were emptying the south bins at the Julian elevator. Three of them, eighteen feet high and fourteen across, corrugated tin cylinders with Chinese-coolie-hat roofs. Had to get at them in high summer when the ground at the south end wasn't too marshy and would hold the truck, Tim's dad said. That milo had been in there seven years, he said, it was turning into dirt.

Tim sat against the side of the bin, in the shade, watching the auger work. It was a big pipe set up on wheels, with a screw inside, sharp and shiny, that pulled the grain in at the bottom end, propelled it up the pipe, and shot it down into the truck with a tremendous racket.

The red dust churned from the truck and hung like disease in the air. It drifted across the road, turning the white gravel red, and coloring the first rows of Wilmer's sweet corn patch with a coppery film. It covered the hood of the truck, the roof, it drifted in through the open windows and settled on the seats, the dash, the black gear shift knob.

When the grain was piled high and almost spilling over on the cab, Tim sprinted into the dust cloud, slid in the seat and cranked the starter. He moved the truck a few feet ahead, shut her off, and went back upwind to the shade. As he waited for the back end to fill, the heavy rumble of the auger changed to a loud clanking. The clanking stopped for a few seconds, then came back, clattering louder than before. His father came running from the office and killed the juice at the breaker box.

"Don't you know nothing? You can't run her empty. You'll burn out the auger bearings."

His father rapped on the steel door above the hole that fed the auger, listening. He opened the highest of three inner doors, and cursed at the musty smell of milo and pesticide that enveloped them. Peering around his father, Tim saw a high circular wall of grain sloping steeply down to the base of the door. The wall was not even, but molded into grotesque formations, with ridges and crevasses and strange, gravity-defying sculptures. It made Tim think of the cartoon landscapes of the roadrunner show. His father leaned inside and poked the wall with his hand. A dusty cascade of milo came down, leaving another intricate wall in its place.

"Dirty, moldy stuff," he muttered. He walked to the truck, took the scoop shovel that hung on the tailgate, and handed it to Tim. "You got to poke it so's it goes down to feed the auger."

When the load was full, Tim shut off the auger and drove the heavy truck to the scale that stretched in front of the grain elevator office like an abbreviated airstrip. He nodded to his father at the desk, moved the big levers of the Fairbanks scale, punched in the weight, and drove around to the main elevator so Wilmer could unload him and put the milo into boxcars bound for Omaha.

Wilmer took a handful as it poured from the tailgate and brought it to his nose. His thin, craggy face screwed up. "Some musty stuff, ain't it?"

"Yeah, Dad says it's getting buggy."

Wilmer grabbed for a shovel to clean out the corners of the truck. "How's your mom?"

"Better," Tim said. "She's doing better."

"Good." The shovel clanged against the corners. Before the next load, Tim ate his lunch in the office, lounging on the daybed while his father worked at his desk and listened to the noon market reports on the radio. Tim liked bologna sandwiches, but Mrs. Booker made them with butter instead of mustard, which made him faintly sick. He never said anything, though. The memory of the Boy Scouts Indian costume was too fresh in his mind, his father wadding it up and asking who did he think he was giving her extra work to do. Mrs. Booker had gone around sullen-faced for days, muttering against his dad.

"Yeah, it sure is hot," Tim said between bites. "But the milo's going like blue thunder. Ought to knock off two bins this afternoon."

His father turned around in the swivel chair, pausing to hawk up and spit in the sack he kept next to the desk. "Let's just make sure we get the one emptied today, okay?"

As milo roared into the truck for the next load, Tim, on tip-toes, leaned inside the bin and poked with his shovel to keep the grain coming down to the auger. He liked doing a man's work, doing it the way his brother did before he went off to college. Somebody had to be there steady. Wilmer missed a lot of days because he was a drunk, and Tim's father took mornings off to go to the hospital.

Tim always thought he'd be the elevator man of the family. He liked to look at the towering silver elevator with its slope-shouldered sides and peaked headhouse. He imagined it as the fortress of the lower half of Julian, locked in struggle with the hill part of town and its guardian water tower. Early in the summer, when he'd overheard his dad talk to a farmer friend of selling the elevator, he'd waited until they were alone, and then tried to say that he could take care of things now and then by himself, but his father had cut him off with a short laugh.

The auger started clanking again, and Tim couldn't reach far enough in to get the grain down. Again his father came running, and Tim cringed in the accusing silence when the auger shut off.

His dad said, "You don't know nothing, damn kid." He yanked the shovel from Tim's hand, reached in the bin and brought more grain down to the auger. He turned the juice back on and yelled above the racket, "You got to climb in there and knock it down. But not too much at a time so's it buries you."

Tim stepped into his father's cupped hands, and was boosted through the opening. He sank to his knees in the sea of tiny kernels. He stabbed gingerly at the wall, bringing down a great dusty waterfall of grain. He waited for it to go down, then collapsed more of the stuck milo. He found that he had to move constantly forward, as if on a treadmill, to keep his feet from drifting down to the whirling teeth of the auger. He dislodged a landslide that buried him to the waist, and it took all his strength to work himself free. With each fall of grain more dust filled the air, and it became difficult to see the upper rim of the grain. The bin was a dark dusty oven, and Tim felt his damp shirt grow heavy with clinging dust. Another cascade, and a thick dark blur flew past his ear, startling him. He turned quickly, in time to see the silhouette of a rat dive into the daylight. His gaze lingered there, finally fastening on the truck, which had milo overflowing on the cab and pouring onto the ground. He scrambled out of the bin, cranked the starter and jerked the truck ahead, with milo showering over the windshield. With the auger off, he cleaned up as much of the spill as he could, thankful that his father hadn't seen it.

Tim brought the truck to the scale and entered the office, covered head to toe with dust. He walked past his father and grabbed the dipper to the water bucket.

"Hey!" said his father. "You're getting milo dirt in the drinkwater. Don't you know nothing? Go dump it out and get us a fresh pail."

Tim looked at the thin film of dust on the water. Protest welled up within him. His father didn't know how hard he worked to move that smelly milo. He yanked the bucket from the shelf and stalked outside to dump it. He went to the well, hung the bucket on the spout, and pumped the long iron handle. Half way back to the office his pant leg brushed the rim and the water was contaminated again. He emptied and refilled again, and carried the heavy bucket painstakingly back to the office. Did his father expect him not to have a drink of water between loads when he was working in that tin furnace? He placed the bucket back on the shelf, faced his father and blurted, "Well, how am I supposed to get a lousy drink then?"

His father slowly took off the dime store bifocals he wore at the desk and looked at Tim. "Drink out of the pump, dummy. And don't let that auger wind out. I can hear it from in here."

Tim parked the truck beneath the auger, then climbed in the bin and scooped a big pile over the auger's mouth. He got out to turn on the machine, and was dismayed to see how quickly it sucked up his work. The slope of grain was no longer steep. He needed to use the shovel more and more to pull it downhill to the auger. Soon he was scooping nonstop. He coughed in the thick dust, the sharp intakes bringing more dust down his throat. Every time he stopped to catch his breath the auger rattled loudly, demandingly, and he could picture the dark look on his father's face. So he scooped, breathing the dust and feeling the layer of black sludge thicken on his clothes and skin.

He didn't bother to fill the back end of the truck. He weighed it and drove into the elevator, where Wilmer gave a low whistle at the sight of him.

"Drink?" Wilmer extended a half-finished bottle of Coke. Tim tasted the grit in his teeth as he drank.

"Go on, finish it. Just makes me wish it was beer anyways." Wilmer grinned, showing his bad teeth, and pulled something from his pocket. "Look here, Tim, an Indian Head nickel. You'll want to keep that for your coin collection."

Tim took it with a weak smile. "Thanks."

Wilmer turned to open the tailgate. "Filthy, dirty stuff ain't fit for man nor beast. Tell you what, Tim. You tell your dad you need a break. I'll take care of the next load. I can finish that boxcar in the morning."

When Tim brought the truck around, Wilmer was waiting by the bin, but Tim, climbing down from the cab, shook his head. "Dad says he promised that boxcar to Cargill tonight. I got to do the load myself."

"Your dad's crazy, Tim." Wilmer started toward the elevator. "You shouldn't be here at all, terrible time like this. You should be home."

Tim watched the back of his hands as he scooped. The sweat ran in his eyes, stinging them, but he had nothing to wipe them with. He found that if he stared at the back of his hands he could keep his eyes in a squint where he didn't have to scratch at them. The hands seemed to take on a life of their own—right on the handle, left on the shaft—as they guided the wide scoop back and forth through the swimming underworld of grain. The noise and heat made him light-headed. He staggered through the grain, pushing scoopfuls to the auger, till at last he looked out and saw the mound of grain climbing above the side of the truck. He clambered out, turned off the auger and sat on the step of the truck, panting and dizzy. He noticed a stinging in his hands, and was surprised to see dirty pink rings of exploded blisters on his palms.

"What are you waiting for, first frost?"

"Have to move the truck," Tim answered, climbing quickly behind the wheel so his father would not see the tears gathering in his eyes. The auger rumbled to life before he was out of the truck, and Tim scrambled to get in and start scooping. The piles of grain were waist-high, and every bit that went to the auger had to be scooped. He pushed the grain to the machine faster and faster, barely keeping up. He coughed and choked, and his hands were on fire. Wilmer's voice echoed in his head. *Your dad's crazy. . . shouldn't be here. . . terrible time.* It came as a shock to realize Wilmer wasn't talking about the milo bin at all. *You should be home.* He could hardly stand being at home when he was there. Wild thoughts raced through his mind. He would hit his dad with the shovel, and he'd run away. He'd take the grain truck and get on the state highway and just keep driving and never come back.

From the back of the bin he thought he saw his father in the doorway, but he couldn't be sure in the brown particulate haze. "Turn it off! Stop it! Stop it!" But his voice was lost in the roar of the auger, and Tim kept scooping.

Finally it stopped. The quiet rang like thunder in his ears as he dragged himself to the door. His father opened the two lower doors and he stumbled through, dropping his shovel in the strange sunlight. Everything was too bright, too crisp, and shimmered at the edges. He held one nostril closed and blew black stringy slime from the other. He coughed, choking on the gobs of black mucus that rolled up from his throat and lungs. He began to panic, retching and gasping for air. A hand held his shoulder and another pounded his back. The retching turned to sobs, and the tears made vertical streaks on his coal miner's face.

"Catch your breath," his father said. "I'll unload. Go get a drink."

Tim walked to the pump, dizzy, sniffling and coughing. His head pounded from the crying, but he couldn't make himself stop. He pumped the handle and splashed cold water on his face, his head, his shoulders. He put his mouth on the spout, drinking gallons, coughing and choking. "I ain't going back in there," he said to himself. "I don't care if he whips me dead, I ain't going in there again."

He stood by the pump a long time, and finally wandered toward the office. He would stand up to his father. He would. He wasn't going back in there. He'd stand quiet and brave and take whatever his father wanted to dish out.

A green car was parked next to the scale. Tim sniffled back his tears as he saw a farm couple, James and Eva Swail, standing inside. They were dressed in city clothes. "Well, Harry," Eva was saying to his dad, "if you don't want to send a trifecta, I guess you'll just miss out. I seen in the paper one of them been paid four hundred dollars." Seeing Tim she laughed and said, "And aren't you a sight? You know, my boys would give anything to get that dirty. You be careful when you play around by the machinery, you hear?"

"I work here," Tim said stiffly.

"Oh, isn't that nice. Well, we're off to Omaha." She paused at the door. "Oh, how is Virginia?"

"Still bedridden," said Tim's father.

"Well, I don't blame her. I'd like to be bedridden myself for a few days to get me out of housework."

Tim's father hawked. He spat in his sack and took one slow step toward the lady. "The cancer's come back," he said quietly, in a voice that frightened Tim. "She's going in for another operation next week, but they don't know if they can do anything. Good enough excuse to get out of housework, you think?" He walked out, slamming the door.

"Well how was I to know?" Eva asked shrilly to the air. She turned to Tim. "When are they doing it? Are they taking her to Omaha again?"

Tim was powerless to speak or move.

James Swail took his wife's elbow, "Come on."

"What? What did I do?" Tim could still hear her as they shuffled across the scale and got in their car. "Not my fault she's dying or whatever. I was just asking."

As Tim walked out to the south bins, he saw Vaughn Jones wheeling the oxygen tank along the gravel street. His old eyes had a devilish gleam as he waved his mail toward the milo bin, where the auger rumbled and dust rolled out of the open door and drifted in the air. "Getting down to the dirty work now, boy," he wheezed, and continued down the road.

Tim found his shovel leaned against the bin. His father was inside the bin with a shovel of his own. As Tim hesitated, a pair of brown work gloves landed at his feet. "Those might help some," came the shout over the auger's roar.

Tim put on the gloves and stepped into the hot dark bin. Father and son bent their backs in the dust and scooped grain. Their feet sank to solid floor, and the bin echoed with the sound of shovels scraping concrete. Tim didn't know who he hated more, his father, old Vaughn, or Eva Swail. For months he had said, mechanically, when anybody asked, that she was doing better, and believed it was true. After all, his mom didn't come near the elevator, never worked in grain dust. It didn't make sense that she wasn't getting better. *Getting down to the dirty work now, boy.*

His father worked with closed mouth, methodically sliding the scoop from pile to auger, pile to auger, never lifting, always sliding. After a time, they turned off the auger. Together they wheeled the machine in, so that its mouth sat at the center of the bin. Tim repositioned the truck, and they began again. They shovelled the last piles to the auger and scraped inward from the walls, using the shovels like brooms. They poured the last scoopfuls down onto the auger's rotating tip, and they shut it off.

They stood on the dusty grass together, blowing brown slime from their noses and hawking it up from their throats. It wasn't spit, but a continuous rope of mucus, and every time you chewed a piece off to spit out, you found yourself gagging on more. As Tim recovered, he became more aware of the violence of his father's pain. He was all bent over, holding his sides, trying to blast air through thirty years of dust. Tim half expected to see blood on the grass.

Finally, his father began to breathe more like normal. He hawked a couple more times, then leaned and picked up his hat from where it had fallen when he was doubled over. He swatted it against his thigh, adjusted it on his head, and used thumb and forefinger to wipe the water from his eyes. He noticed Tim looking at him, and gave a hard smile. "So you want to be an elevator man," he said. "Let's get to it then. We got two more bins to empty by Friday."

❦

Chapter Two

Writing From The Heart

THINK ABOUT SEX. While it is possible to do it all by oneself, most people consider it more significant and more satisfying with a partner. And in order to achieve the best results, it's generally considered a good strategy to put the needs of the partner first.

So it is with the writer and the reader of fiction. You can write for yourself alone, but most writers find more satisfaction in creating an effect upon readers. As you orient yourself to the task of story writing, it's a good idea to consider the needs and desires of your readers.

Never forget that your first and biggest challenge is to keep them reading. That means the first sentence must hook the reader's interest, the second must build on that interest, and so on. At or near the end of the story, whatever forces have been creating that interest should come to some kind of showdown or resolution that will give the reader a satisfying sense of completeness. This progression, called the plot, is often depicted as a triangle:

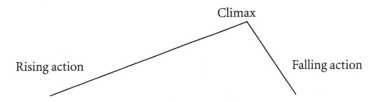

Plot (what happens) and character (to whom it happens) are both essential to stories. Beginning writers have a tendency to start by dreaming up a catchy plot—the home team wins the big game, the jewel thief ends up stealing cubic zirconium, the pet raccoon turns out to have rabies—with character development as a secondary concern. These plots often depend on a "surprise" ending to give the story its pay-off, to make the story worthwhile—as in the plot ideas mentioned above. But surprise endings are difficult to manage, and can easily err either on the side of predictability ("I saw it coming way before the end") or implausibility ("Why did it end that way? It doesn't make sense"). Anyway, if the reader doesn't care about the characters involved, she won't care whether the raccoon has rabies or babies. Many "surprise" endings have been done so often they lack the ability to surprise. You would be well advised, for example, not to bother concocting a story that ends, "and then I woke up."

The Primacy of Character

In constructing your first stories, it will be more productive to think first of characters, and let the plot work itself out in accordance with what these characters would do in this situation. If you give your readers real people, with real concerns and desires and problems, the readers will be interested in practically anything the characters do.

Good character development has plot opportunities waiting at every corner. A story that begins, "Beth has a problem. Last night Keith said he couldn't stand goldfish," opens up all kinds of questions for the reader. Who's Beth? Who's Keith, and what's he got against goldfish? Answering those questions about the characters will set off a chain of events that can be shaped into a plot. Keith may convince Beth to disown her goldfish, or she may have to get a restraining order to keep him from eating them. In any case, unless the author makes us care about Beth and Keith, we won't care how it turns out.

Climax

But what does that mean, "how it turns out"? In the case of Beth and Keith, it may be the moment Beth falls in love with him, or the moment she sees that his antipathy for goldfish signals a general nastiness of character. In both cases, notice that it is Beth's change of mind that constitutes the defining moment, or the "climax" of the story's plot. The Irish author James Joyce borrowed the religious term "epiphany" to describe the moment in which the character gains a new understanding of a person or a situation. A change of heart, or of mind, a moment of new insight, or even a turning away from new insight, can be an epiphanic moment that will provide a satisfying sense of completion to a short story.

To be effective, an epiphany does not have to be of the order of the pagan Saul getting knocked off his horse by a lightning bolt and becoming the Christian Paul. In one of the most famous examples, Joyce's "Araby," a young boy realizes that he will not be able to keep his promise to buy a gift for a girl, and suddenly sees himself "as a creature driven and derided by vanity."

Even from this brief quote, you can see that the epiphany in "Araby" is a painful one. This is, sadly, how many of our realizations occur in real life. We suffer setbacks more often than we triumph. Hopes are dashed, plans go awry, good guys finish last.

Another Irish writer, Frank O'Connor, has made a strong case that throughout its history, the short story form has been suited best to the expression of loneliness, of loss, of marginalization.

We all have a part of ourselves that is insecure; we have times when we feel like outcasts. Our hearts go out more readily to people in pain. You will stand a better chance of making an emotional connection with your reader if you write about hard times than if you write about good times.

Even if you want your story to end happily, your readers will be more satisfied with the outcome if your characters have had to overcome obstacles and earn their happiness. Encountering those obstacles, and the doubts they raise, constitutes the rising action of the plot. If your character sails through on a wave of triumph and bliss, from the story's beginning to its end, you risk boring your reader with the lack of complication, or, worse, gaining her resentment.

Closure

At the end of your story, how neatly you tie up all the loose ends is up to you. Many contemporary readers prefer a more ragged ending, with little if any of the plot tensions resolved. A tendency to focus on surfaces, leave out psychological development of characters, and break off the story climax or closure are characteristics of certain writers who are sometimes called "minimalists." In the hands of a masterful technician like Raymond Carver or Ann Beattie, such stories can be exquisitely beautiful and penetrating. But the risks are obvious. The reader can feel cheated, or find the story unshaped or unfinished. The writer should seek feedback from the workshop on this important point, to find out what level of closure is most satisfying to readers of a particular story.

Final Effect

What, in the end, should your story do to a reader? Amuse? Entertain? Inspire? Outrage? It depends on the story, of course, but two things are clear: you want to create *some* emotional response, and you'd like it to be more or less the response that you, as writer, intend. I think the best you can strive for is what I call the "tuning fork effect." A tuning fork, when struck, produces an audible vibration. When it is held near another tuning fork, the second one catches the vibrations of the first, producing a similar sound. If your story, at its emotional center, can produce a sympathetic vibration in the heart of your reader, so that the reader feels the emotional processes and they become a part of her, you have accomplished something rare and wonderful. The best stories I read are the ones that make me cry. That doesn't mean all good stories are gut-wrenching tragedies. My tears may come from joy, pain, love, loss, triumph, or a host of other emotional states. The trick is that the emotions are authentic.

The Subject Matter Inside Yourself

There is a tendency for beginning writers to feel that their own lives are boring, that they must invent grandiose adventures in order to capture a reader's imagination. Not so. There is no such thing as boring subject matter, only boring ways of writing about it. Yes, there are highly dramatic wife-on-safari-blows-husband's-head-off-with-elephant-gun stories ("The Short Happy Life of Francis McComber" by Ernest Hemingway), but there are a lot more stories about homely everyday life.

You do not have to go on safari to find something worth writing about. You have to go somewhere a lot scarier: the innermost reaches of your own heart. There's an old proverb that says an artist must suffer. A mentor of mine once told me that, to him, it means an artist must be willing to scrape his or her rawest nerves, must be willing to open the doors on the emotional hiding places.

It takes great courage to lay open the fears and disappointments of your life, but it is in dealing with such things honestly that you have the best hope to create that sympathetic vibration in the soul of your reader. Hemingway also wrote a story in which a man does nothing but sit at a bar feeling lost, lonely and fearful, and "A Clean, Well-Lighted Place" is considered by many to be his masterpiece.

To make an omelet, as the saying goes, you have to break a few eggs. To make a story, you have to break open some parts of yourself that may have been sealed off for a long time. It takes courage. It takes honesty. And, unfortunately, when you manage to do it, you won't automatically have a short story. Just as an omelet has more ingredients than cracked eggs, so a short story has more ingredients than the heartfelt revelation of one's inner life.

This can be a difficult truth for any writer to accept. The very process of putting down on paper what's been kept penned up can be highly emotional, highly cathartic. (*Catharsis*, another word from Aristotle, refers to the sudden rush of pent-up emotions you feel when you see a movie, a play, or read a book that really gets to you.) When the writing creates such strong emotions in us, we are tempted to believe it will twang the tuning fork in everybody, and that we have therefore written a great work of art. The trouble is that we are in no position to judge. At the moment of childbirth, *all* babies are the most beautiful geniuses the world has ever seen. The writer must get some distance, some perspective, in order to make an intelligent evaluation of her work. For most writers, this means a physical removal—get away from the story, think about other things. When she comes back to it, she must be a different person. The anxious parent must become the hard-eyed mechanic. She must fully expect the need to cut and add, to rearrange and shape, in order to turn her first draft into a story that appeals to a wider audience.

This is a whole different process, but it too can be painful, as is graphically suggested in another old saying, that a writer must learn to kill her babies. What that means is, a writer on many occasions will need to change or rearrange or take out the very things that were most meaningful to her in the first writing in order to make the story more meaningful for her readers.

The kind of storymaking I'm describing here should remind you of the Greek philosophers mentioned in the previous chapter. Writing what happened to you is writing history. When you shape the incidents so that they have relevance and meaning to your reader too—when you universalize them—then you are writing stories that may be called a kind of poetry. And poetry, Aristotle tells us, because it is universal rather than particular, is a higher thing than history.

The Subject Matter Outside Yourself

About now, some of you are saying, "Whoa, wait a minute. I came to this class to write fiction, not to slit my wrists. What about fantasy and science fiction? What about war stories, cop stories, historical romance?"

These are called genre fictions, and although they may sound like fun and they may seem easy, they hold many hidden traps for the beginning writer. When you attempt these purely fabricated stories, you may find that you are not invested in the characters, and that you aren't familiar enough with the realistic details that you need to be convincing. Additionally, each genre operates within a set of informal rules, or conventions, that are complex and particular. There are how-to books available for every genre. If you try a genre story with only a casual understanding of what it entails, the result may look more like poor parody than the real thing.

The genre that I am advocating might be called autobiographically-based psychological realism. Because it is closest to experience, it is the one that beginning writers have the best chance to pull off with some success. I've had students say they don't want to write stories out of their own lives because it's "too easy." They quickly discover what a large misconception that is. No story is ever easy. Every good writer I know has tales of botched attempts, beginnings that fizzled, ideas that went nowhere.

There is incontestable wisdom in the oldest, most common rag of advice: write what you know. Your experiences and your emotions. If you don't feel the anger or the elation or the compassion your character is supposed to possess on paper, then chances are your reader won't feel it either. Genre stories require believable well-rounded characters and good plotting, but they also require a familiarity with genre conventions, and, often, as with crime fiction, a specific area of knowledge.

Remember, Hemingway had been on safari, so he had the details at hand to make such stories authentic. But we all have areas of experience and expertise that we can mine for details to give our stories texture and authority. It may seem boring to you that your job is to empty the quarters from parking meters, or to re-check the expense vouchers of junior executives, or to maintain the sprinkler system of a golf course, but your knowledge of the intricacies of the job can bring vibrancy and life to your stories that you could never accomplish trying to make up a convincing safari or hostile corporate takeover.

I once had a student who was seriously involved with reenactments of Civil War battles. He had his own uniform and musket. He had participated in a great number of stagings, including Gettysburg and Antietam. Out of this experience, he wanted to write a story set during the Civil War. In his story, the battlefield descriptions were vivid and believable. However, when he shifted the action back to the barracks, his story fell flat. Although he was the same age as his Yankee soldier protagonist, he had no inkling of that character's true experience. The mortal terror of a true battlefield, the heavy responsibility of a young wife waiting at home. At my suggestion, his next story was set at a Civil War reenactment. This story turned out to be more believable and more successful. Although it did not have the gravity of the real Civil War, this story did create a fascinating behind-the-scenes glimpse into the world of the reenactment. Here he was writing from what he knew.

If what you are really interested in writing is science fiction, or some other genre, I suggest you think of this class as a tune-up, as a warm-up. All of the skills you develop here will be eminently applicable to whatever genre you choose to try later. In the meantime, you can take a tip from the Civil War buff. Try writing a story about a *character* who is a science fiction fanatic, or a fan of cop shows, or someone who has read too many romances.

Prewriting Exercises

So you've decided to write your first story based on some experience of your own life. Which one? Where to start? There is no time when the computer screen looks so blank, the paper so white, as when you sit down to write the first line of your first short story. All your great ideas, all your motivation and ambition get sucked in to the vortex of emptiness. At this point, you might be tempted to decide that you are not inspired, and should put off writing the story until the muse touches you.

That may work, but chances are it won't. Your memory holds more than you think it does. And it likes to play tricks on you, concealing that which it doesn't want to give out. Before you try to write your first narrative as a story, you might try some guided memory exercises. I provide a couple of samples, as follow. They may be done in the classroom or at home, but they are most effective with a guide; that is, with someone reading or speaking the instructions out loud, leaving the writer free to visualize. The setting should be calm. There should be no hurry.

1. "Look Homeward Angel"

Try to be calm. Clear your mind of all thoughts. Concentrate on yourself sitting there, at your desk, doing nothing. Picture yourself there, how you look. Now in your imagination rise up out of the chair. Visualize yourself rising right through the roof of the building you are in. Look down on it. Now rise higher in the sky, look down on the campus, the town, and begin to fly, back to your old home town. Keep visualizing. There is your town. You're looking at it from the sky. What do you see? Picture it. Travel to your home. Look at it from the sky. What does it look like? Travel slowly down to your back yard, or your front yard, noting all details. Pass into the house. At first it seems there's nobody home, so just look at the details. The furniture, the walls, the rug. Things lying around. Go from room to room. Note what you see there. Pay attention to the colors of things, and the textures. Are there any smells? Any sounds? Ah, someone is there after all. In the hallway or in the kitchen. You see that person now. Who is it? What does she look like? What is he wearing? What expression is on his or her face? Study it closely. What is this person doing? What is this person concerned about? Is this person you? Or are you also in the house? Yes, there you are. What is your relation to the other person or persons here? How old is the you that you are seeing? What were your concerns then? Linger over all of these details. What are the people in this vision saying? What are they doing? Pay attention, this is important!

Now, take up your pen or keyboard, and write. Everything. Start anywhere. Don't analyze or interpret, don't worry about phrasing or chronology or background explanations. Just write. Just record the contents of your vision. You'll figure out what to do with it later. For now, just let your fingers be faucets, and pour out everything you've seen. Write for ten or twenty or thirty minutes. Write until exhausted.

2. Epiphanic Moment

Recall a moment of personal interaction with someone you know in which you were surprised, caught off guard, embarrassed, or disappointed. Picture the exact moment that this emotion hit you. Where were you? What does this setting look like? Picture it, with as many colors and textures and details as you can muster. Who was the other person? What was the subject you were talking about? What were the exact words, or the movement or gesture that caused you surprise, caught you off guard, embarrassed or disappointed you? Replay that single minute, paying attention to all details. What were the exact words exchanged? What inflections of voice, look, or mannerisms attended the moment? Relive it. Now, it's probably the case that you shouldn't have been surprised by whatever it was. There were clues, weren't there? You just missed them. In retrospect, the words or actions of this person were completely typical of him or her, or atypical in an explainable way. Think about these reasons, this explanation. Was anyone else there? What was his or her take on what happened? If no one else was there, who is the most relevant third party? How would she or he hear about it, and what would he or she say? How would that interpretation be different from yours? Describe why that person would have a different take, or a different allegiance. Again, think it all first, then write it all down. All of it, as fast as you can, as much as you can, without shaping, without worry. Just dump it on the page.

A Note to Teachers:

These guided memory exercises are powerful instruments, and should not be undertaken lightly. Painful memories can be unearthed, and it is not unusual to have someone break into tears in the process of reliving the pain. I have spoken of the courage and honesty it takes to write a compelling story. The products of these exercises are not stories, and decorum should be observed. No one should ever be coerced into reading or revealing what these exercises have produced. Revelations should be voluntary. Sometimes the outpourings are too painful to touch, and the writer is not capable of transforming this exercise into a story. Those feelings should be respected.

A Note to Students:

While what you write in these exercises may be too painful or too private to share, and others must respect that, you should not immediately burn them or seal them up in a vault as forever untouchable. It often happens that if you set them aside for awhile, let the images and memories percolate, that you come up with a way of seeing it, a way of using it, that you didn't have before. Just a line, or an image, or a slice of scene can provide the genesis for a story that hits close to the emotional core of your life without betraying too much of your privacy.

At the other end of the spectrum, you must not fall in love with your outpourings and consider them to be a finished story. Just because they are heartfelt and powerful to you does not make their power immediately accessible to your readers. Do not insist on their artistic purity, having been torn from your bleeding breast. Be willing to acknowledge that it may take a lot of changing and shaping to fashion a story out of your memories.

Now it is time for you to put this book aside for awhile, to turn inward and find the part of yourself that needs to be written about. Now it is time for you to let loose a story into the world.

Chapter Three

Rewriting With The Mind

CONGRATULATIONS. You've written your first story. It's based on something from your own experience, and you're pretty sure it has some kind of rising action, a climax, and a denouement. Now you want to change it and shape it to make it have a tuning fork effect on your readers, produce a catharsis that offers a satisfying sense of closure, but not too much closure. Fine. What now?

What do I mean by these constant references to changing and shaping? I mean the mechanical decisions about what words you choose, and in what order. In writing your first draft, most of these choices are unconscious, intuitive. In order to rewrite, you must be able to identify the choices you've made, and consider alternatives.

Person, Tense, Point of View

At the most basic level, you have two choices of person, first and third, and two choices of tense, past and present. Either of the former will work with either of the latter. The main thing is, once you make your choice, stick to it. For example, the same opening sentence could be written in any of these ways:

I wonder if Joe will still be mad at me tonight.
(1st person, present tense)

Trish wonders if Joe will still be mad at her tonight.
(3rd person, present tense)

I wondered if Joe would still be mad at me tonight.
(1st person, past tense)

Trish wondered if Joe would still be mad at her tonight.
(3rd person, past tense)

Note that the third person can be just as intimate as the first; that is, the reader is privileged to know what Trish thinks and feels. Usually it is better to limit this mind-reading privilege to one character, the protagonist. This is called *limited omniscient* point of view, and is like a first-person story in that the reader is permitted to see the thoughts and feelings of the main character, and nobody else. If we begin the second sentence, "Joe was mad all right," conveying this information directly to the reader, not filtered through Trish's perspective ("Joe was mad all right; when he called Trish had to hold the receiver away from her ear"), then we have *omniscient* point of view.

In terms of tense, note that past and present refer only to verb tense, not to when the story takes place. The traditional storytelling voice employs the past tense, but still conveys a sense of immediacy. The story seems to be unfolding as you read it.

Foreground and Background

Writing a story is like the juggling act in which you keep a dozen china plates spinning atop sticks, all at once. As juggler, you have to run back and forth like mad among the plates, giving another spin to each before it slows and falls. When you begin a short story, you set a lot of plates spinning, and you must not neglect them. In the foreground, you have the main character, her immediate tensions and concerns as they play themselves out in particular times (*scenes*) and places (*settings*). But this action must unfold against a realistic background world that gives the reader a wider sense of setting and situation.

In a story that begins with Trish wondering if Joe will still be mad at her tonight, the obvious question is, What caused Joe to be mad at her in the first place? This presents a problem to the writer of how much *exposition* to include, whether to use a flashback to let the reader see the source of the tension, whether to present it via Trish's thoughts about it, or whether to let the reader guess and keep the story moving forward from there, with only such pertinent clues as come out of the ensuing interaction of Trish and Joe.

In general, it is preferable to try to keep *exposition* to a minimum, and keep the story moving forward. But there are other background aspects that may need to be addressed. Where is this taking place? Within the first two paragraphs a story should locate the action with some details of *setting*. It also may be relevant to include Trish's job, or her age, or her self-image. How much background information is necessary? There is no right answer to that question. Good writers find ways to work salient background points into the foreground of the story.

A Couple of Caveats

One common mistake of first-time story writers is to overestimate how much material they can fit into a short story, how much time they can cover. If it's the story of a love affair that ends, a student writer will typically think she needs to begin when the lovers meet. She writes for twenty pages, and finds her characters are still on their first date. They haven't even had a tiff yet, much less broken up. Better to start with the break-up itself, and find out how much you'll need to go back and fill in with preliminary details. Notice that both of the prewriting exercises in the previous chapter do that: they start with the crucial point, the climax, and work from there.

Another common problem is too many characters. In most short stories, you only have time to develop two or three characters. If you start bringing in a whole pack of buddies, plus their parents, you will often find that they are just names, with no real identity or purpose in the story. Get rid of them, or give them a limp. By "limp," writers mean that a character, however minor, must have some distinguishing quality. It could be something the character always says or always wants, something the character wears, a nickname, or something in the way a character looks.

An important function of minor characters is to reveal more about the major characters. Thus it is useful to set up contrasts. If the protagonist's flaw is indecisiveness, write his friend to be wildly impetuous. Shakespeare shows Laertes hell-bent for revenge when *his* father is killed, a contrast that sharpens the picture of the over-scrupulous Hamlet. When a character is used to contrast another character, either one may be referred to as the *foil* of the other.

The Importance of Scene

What I call the *foreground* of the story comprises those parts that are presented as *scenes*. These are the actions that are presented directly to the reader, as if on stage, for the reader to see, hear, taste, touch, smell and feel things as they occur. What I call *background* may also be called *narration* or *exposition*. These are places where the writer fills in needed details about the situation at hand, or where an action is condensed or summarized for the reader.

Part of the challenge of constructing a good story is deciding where to use scene, and where to use narration. Scenes have many advantages. In scenic presentation, the reader gets to experience most fully the action of the story. However, scenes take up a lot of space. Often, it is more economical to use narration. A general rule of thumb is that the more important the part of the story is, the more obligated you are to use scene to show that part happening. Since the climax is a very important part of the story, some writers refer to it as the *obligatory scene*. If you fail to deliver the promised scene, the result can be disappointing to the reader, or, worse, unintentionally funny.

Say, for example, that your story's narrator has to meet his boss at five-thirty. All day he worries about the meeting. He hopes the boss hasn't noticed how he messed up the Excalibur account. On the other hand, he coaches the boss's son in Little League, and their last game, scheduled for tonight, has been postponed by rain. Maybe it's just about that. Throughout the day, our narrator catches glimpses of the boss here and there, and speculates on what the meeting will bring. If the story ends, "I went to see the boss and she said I was doing great and gave me a raise, so my worrying was pointless," then the reader is likely to feel that the story itself was pointless. The story has made an implicit promise to the reader that she'll be able to see what happens at that five-thirty appointment. And the writer is obligated to deliver. If the narrator is going to get a raise, we're entitled to hear the words and feel the handshake. Why else have we been made to follow him around all day?

On the other hand, we probably don't have to follow him to the washroom, know what he had for lunch, or learn how he found out about the Little League game, unless these incidents have direct relevance to what happens at the end. For example:

At eleven-thirty his phone beeped. He picked up the receiver. His secretary said, "Joe, your wife's on the phone."

"Okay, put her on." He waited for the click, and then said, "Hi, hon."

"Hi. How's your day?"

"All right. I'm nervous about the meeting with Hollings at five-thirty."

"I know. I hope it's not anything bad. I just wanted to let you know that the game tonight has been postponed because of the rain."

"Yeah, okay. Did they say if it was rescheduled?"

"They said tomorrow if it lets up."

"Okay. Thanks for calling."

"Bye."

"Bye." Joe replaced the receiver in its cradle.

Whew. That's ten separate chunks of dialogue, mostly consisting of niceties ("Bye"), and what we presumably already know (that Joe is worried), all to get out one bit of marginally relevant plot detail, that the Little League game has been cancelled. If the writer is going to include all that, she should capitalize on the opportunity to give us some insight into Joe, his wife, or their relationship ("Joe, you promised to ease up. If you make those kids do push-ups again half of them are going to quit."). If the conversation is unimportant, throw it all out in favor of an economical bit of narration:

At eleven-thirty his wife called to tell him the little league game had been postponed.

My story "The Elevator Man" (in Chapter 1) begins with exposition, two paragraphs that introduce characters by giving their perspectives on the repugnance of various kinds of grain dust. Even then, bits of scenic presentation are smuggled in (". . . Vaughn Jones pointed to the cloud of red dust rising . . .") to allow the reader more direct experience. The third paragraph employs setting as a transition to plunge the reader into the first scene. Most of the rest of the story is played out in scenes.

Dialogue

Dialogue is crucial to most short stories. It is where your characters get to come alive, to speak for themselves. Bad dialogue drags a story down. Good dialogue elevates it. In order to learn to write dialogue, a writer must develop her ear. Listen to people, how they talk, what they say. Go to a diner or mall and eavesdrop on strangers. Imagine how the words they speak to each other would look if typed on a page.

In the mechanical presentation, it is easiest on the reader if you begin a new paragraph each time you change speakers. That means you may have a one-word paragraph, as in

"No."

which is fine. Do not automatically begin the new paragraph with the quotation itself, but rather, think of a camera. Change paragraphs when the camera swings from one person to another.

"Dance with me," I said to the woman in overalls.
She looked up from her knitting and smiled. "My boyfriend carries a switchblade."

In this example, the change of paragraph occurs between "overalls" and "She"; that is, at the moment the attention swings from the narrator to the woman. If the new paragraph started where her actual dialogue begins, it would be confusing, leading the reader to think perhaps someone else is speaking.

A writer must be careful not to try to sneak too much background information into dialogue. In real life, people don't often say what both parties already know, as in,

"Good night, Elizabeth Ann Mulhaney, to whom I've been married for six years. It sure is peaceful in our split-level home here in Valley Forge, fifteen miles from Philadelphia. Sleep well."

Also, be careful not to needlessly interpret the dialogue for the reader, as in,

Karen didn't kiss him when he came in the door. She said, "I don't know. I've been bummed out all day."
Rob could tell something was wrong. "Is it your mother?" he asked.

Well, *of course* he could tell something was wrong. She just told him. Better to go straight to his response, which moves the story forward rather than dwelling on what everybody already knows.

Dialogue Mechanics

Dialogue tags are the small he-said, she-said appendages to dialogue that let the reader know who has spoken, and sometimes how the person has spoken. Beginners often think that it's a good idea to think up creative alternatives to "said," but such creativity often backfires, drawing unwelcome comic attention to the dialogue tags, as in,

"Are you there?" he questioned seriously.
"Sometimes," she quipped cleverly.
"Well, sometimes isn't good enough," he threatened viciously.
"Don't threaten me. Let's talk it out," she expostulated.
"Talk it out?" he sputtered furiously.
"Yes, talk it out," she responded evenly.

The heavy-handed use of dialogue tags, both the verbs and the adverbs here, contribute to overwrought, overexplained, badly-written dialogue. If all the dialogue tags were eliminated, this exchange would be much much better. The emotions attached to each line would still be suggested, but the reader wouldn't be hammered over the head by them. In general, if it's clear who is speaking, dispense with the dialogue tag altogether.

The dialogue should convey its own emotions; they shouldn't have to be stated by the writer. Adverbs should only be appended to dialogue tags when they come as a surprise. Consider, for example, the following two lines,

"Go straight to hell," she said angrily.

"Go straight to hell," she said cheerfully.

In the first example, "angrily" merely repeats the emotion that already came through clearly in the dialogue itself. It is redundant. In the second, however, "cheerfully" catches us by surprise, adds an interesting twist to the sentiment.

Dialogue tags should not call attention to themselves, but melt into the background. Don't be afraid to use "said" ("says" in a present tense story) again and again.

When using alternatives to "said," be sure to consider whether the verb actually describes the delivery of the dialogue, or if it refers to something else the speaker does. For example, a person cannot "grin" a sentence. One can grin before or after speaking a sentence. The difference is in the punctuation:

Wrong: *"I'll go with you," she grinned.*

Right: *"I'll go with you." She grinned.*

Showing and Telling

One of the oldest and wisest bits of advice for story writers is "Show, don't tell." That is, in trying to convey a scene or emotion to your reader, present the details of situation that give rise to the emotion, rather than telling the reader what to feel.

Let's say I just heard a funny one-liner. I can tell you that I laughed. I can describe the quality and timbre of my laugh and tell you it was a really good joke that made me laugh. What is your response? Probably a polite acknowledgement that I found something funny. But if I want to make you laugh, I'll probably have better luck if I ask if you've heard about the three-legged dog who limped into Dodge City and said, "I'm looking for the man who shot my paw."

The point is obvious when applied to telling jokes, but beginning short story writers (and especially poets!) often expect the reader to experience the loneliness, the fear, or the elation of the character simply by telling the reader, sometimes in great detail, that the character is feeling these things. This is likely to win a polite acknowledgement from the reader, but not to tingle the tuning fork of her own loneliness. As with telling the joke, you must recreate the stimulus which caused the emotion, not describe the emotion itself.

Writing with sensual details allows the reader to participate more fully in the action and in the emotions. Let us go back to an example used above.

> *"Dance with me," I said to the woman in overalls.*
> *She looked up from her knitting and smiled. "My boyfriend carries a switchblade."*

I could have had her say, "My boyfriend would be jealous." That would tell the reader the situation. But the switchblade is much more fun, and shows the reader a lot more about the situation. It gives the reader a concrete picture, suggests the possibility of violence, and adds a curious twist to the fact that she is smiling.

You can tell your reader, "Rita was mad." But from this description, the reader learns nothing about Rita's anger, if indeed it is anger, and not insanity. The writer must ask herself how she can show Rita being angry. Is Rita the kind of person who scowls and gives short answers, or the kind who shouts and breaks things? In showing her anger, you are developing her character as well.

In early drafts of "The Elevator Man," I faced the problem of how to engender sympathy for the father, specifically for his grief, which is an essential complement to his hard-nosed surface. I could tell the reader, but that would risk violating the rather more limited awareness of my adolescent narrator. Instead, I hit upon the character of Eva Swail, whose callous questions embody the stupidity and indifference of the outside world, and force the father to speak the unspeakable: his wife is dying.

The Role of the Workshop

None of the particular points in this chapter should be taken as an iron-clad rule. Each writer develops her own writing habits and re-writing instincts over time. You will always be in the process of creating and revising your own theories on how to achieve the best fictive effects. Every choice is situational. You have to ask yourself what would work best at this particular moment for this particular story. That's why the workshop is such a wonderful tool for learning to write.

Students, tearing their first stories straight from the fabric of their lives, find it difficult to view the work as a separate entity, creating all of its own background as it goes, and not having the assumed background of the writer's life to give it context and depth. What the teacher can do, and what students must learn to do for themselves and for their peers in the workshop, is develop the rewriter's eye. That is, they must develop a separate self, a writer self, outside the character who experienced the emotion, and select the ingredients of the story and mix them together in the most effective way.

Writing first drafts is done mainly with the heart. It takes courage, honesty, intensity and trust to tear a living narrative from the tissue of your life. Rewriting is done mainly with the brain. It takes a fine, cold, detached intellect to look at what was produced in the first draft and set about changing and shaping it to make story out of autobiography or, in Aristotle's terms, to make poetry out of history.

Chapter Four

Creating An Effective Workshop

THE HEART of the fiction workshop is the discussion of individual stories. The tone of that discussion and the atmosphere in which it is conducted are almost as important as what is said. The workshop atmosphere can be prone to extremes. At one end of the spectrum are sadists and masochists who believe it must be a ritual of pain. They tend to subscribe to metallurgic metaphors—only in the white hot blast furnace of scorn and contempt can fiction be purged of its manifold impurities and emerge with the hard (and hard-won) gleam of the true metal, the right stuff.

I disagree strongly with that approach. It inflicts gratuitous damage. Some students' gains are offset by the pain and wrecked confidence of others. Furthermore, it tends to promote the false notion that having survived the trial somehow equates to immanent skill and imminent success as a writer.

At the other end of the spectrum is a workshop decorated with the lace doilies of the mutual admiration society. In deference to each other's feelings, teacher and students dissemble their true opinions into non-offensive platitudes of praise. This approach can be greatly encouraging, but the writer who wants to make substantive improvements on a manuscript can be left with little to go on. These workshops are like those death-by-chocolate concoctions at fancy dessert places, delicious at first, but after a few bites you're gagging on the sweetness, and you leave the joint feeling fat and undernourished.

Let us say, then, that the ideal workshop operates in a comfortable if slightly tense space somewhere between the two extremes outlined above. Workshops should be frank but never brutal, encouraging but not falsely congratulatory. Workshopping a story should be a fascinating, complex, interpersonal play of voices that leaves the writer with an enlarged sense of what is happening in her story—its problems, its possibilities, its particular glint of genius.

Different Roles

The workshop is a game of tag: the players take turns being "it." And just as in the game, the rules apply to you differently when you are "it," that is, when your work is being discussed, than when you are not "it." In the following three sections, I address first the role of the reader/responder. Secondly, I discuss how the writer can get the most benefits from having her story workshopped. Finally, I offer some procedural tips to make the thing run more smoothly.

The Ten Commandments of Workshop Criticism

I. Thou art in the workshop neither to praise Caesar nor to bury him, but to help him along to the next draft.
The very presence of the story in the workshop means that it is not finished, and should not be treated as a finished work. Although some stories will be more evolved that others, it is important to discuss every story as a work-in-progress. If you start treating them as finished products, your workshop quickly falls into something that approximates a Siskel-and-Ebert approach to the movies: thumbs up or thumbs down, and then defend the direction of your thumb with catchy praise or insightful criticism. Such a workshop may be entertaining, but it is not nearly as helpful to the writer.

II. The good in a story shall take precedence over the bad.
Remember that in its literary definition, "criticism" does not equal "fault finding," but rather it refers to close analysis of the text from a wide variety of perspectives. This latter is the sense in which a workshop should offer "criticism" of someone's story. A writer needs to know how it made you feel and what it made you think; she needs to know what associative chords she has managed to touch in your life. It is at least as important for a writer to know what is working well and why as it is for a writer to hear what may need fixing. And it is always possible to find something good, and something *potentially* good, in every story. There is no such thing as a totally hopeless story. Yes, I

have seen poorly written stories, poorly conceived stories, but I have never seen a story that didn't hold some line, some sentence, some idea, where glimmered the spark of real life.[1] It can be hard work to find the honestly positive aspect of the story upon which the author can build, but as a good critic, that's your job.

III. The workshop shall be a conversation, not between writer and readers, but among readers, with the writer listening in.

That means that a reader must always listen to what the other readers are saying, and be prepared to agree, disagree, clarify, or offer alternative readings. If one reader plainly misreads a passage, it is incumbent upon other readers to offer corrections, or alternatives, especially since, as I will soon argue, the writer should not jump in to explain, justify, or rebut.

IV. Thou shalt only partially remember The Golden Rule.

Some workshoppers feel that because they themselves welcome harsh, exacting criticism of their works, they therefore have the right to do unto others the same way. That reasoning is spurious. A workshop will have different individuals with different levels of sensitivity. Through personal interaction, a reader must attempt to discern the comfort level of her various partners in the workshop. A reader has neither the right nor the duty to push beyond that writer's comfort level.

V. Thou shalt not commit the Authorial Fallacy.

The great thing about fiction is that it allows a person to deal with the most intimate matters of the heart, the most confessional subjects, the wildest thoughts, and yet remain outside of the matter. As a reader, the extent to which a fictive event is drawn from real life is not relevant, and none of your business. It is never appropriate to ask the writer, "Did that really happen?" or "Is that really you?" or "Do you really believe that?"

---

1   In a story that aims for psychological realism, that is. Failed genre stories, where the author is attending neither to the basics of storymaking nor to an accurate understanding of the demands of the genre, leave me with nothing to advise except, as gently as possible, back to the drawing board. Agent X19's bloody adventures on asteroid B12, for example. Let me say, as loudly as I can shout in a footnote: **Beginning Writers Should Stick With Real Stories of Real People.** Save the genre attempts for the advanced class.

You must respect the fictive veil, even in the way you talk about stories. If a story is written in the first person, readers should always talk about "the narrator" or "the protagonist" and never refer to the character, while speaking to the writer, as "you." It's all right to address the writer *as writer* in the second person, as in, "It's good drama that you chose to have your narrator enter the apartment at the exact moment the statistician was swallowing the goldfish." But it's *not* okay to say, "You came in right when that guy was eating your goldfish. That must have been so weird for you!"

VI. Thou shalt grant the author her givens.

As a reader you are, to some extent, obligated to accept the world the author presents to you, and not take issue with its basic premises or impose your own morality or sensibility on the author's fictive world or her characters. For example, it's not a valid criticism to say, about a character, "Mary shouldn't drink when she's pregnant—that's so bad for the baby!" However, it may well be helpful to question whether it's worth it for the author to sacrifice so much audience sympathy for Mary by having her drink when she's pregnant.

This is a tricky commandment. It is, on one hand, part of a reader's duty to speak up about implausibilities in a story, as in, "It seems improbable to me that an intruder would eat someone's pet goldfish." But having pointed that out, the reader should offer suggestions as to how the writer can account for the odd circumstance, rather than telling the writer not to have that feature in the story.

VII. Thou shalt speak thy mind with great humility and tact.

Remember that the writer has the right to write anything she wants into a story. A reader cannot tell her what to change, a reader can only make suggestions. Don't say, "You've got to change the Colonel. The Colonel is totally unbelievable." Instead, say, "If this were my story, I might do something else with the Colonel," and then go on to make specific suggestions. Criticisms should be addressed to parts rather than to the whole. Instead of labelling a story as "boring," a reader should find the passages where the pace is slow or the action tepid, and make concrete suggestions for how to liven them up.

VIII. Thou shalt not waste time belaboring editing or manuscript flaws.
Workshop time is too valuable to spend pointing out misspelled words or correcting punctuation. Make a note of it, do the writer the courtesy of bringing it to her attention, but don't waste time agreeing all around the table that "misogynist" has a "y" in it.

IX. Thou shalt be sensitive to the tenor of the discussion.
A reader should gauge the overall mood and content of the discussion of every story. If much praise has been heaped, find something to offer a suggestion about. If the story's been taking it on the chops, find something to admire. If a significant part or aspect of the story has not been touched upon, bring it up.

X. Thou shalt not pull rank.
If thou art the teacher, thou mayest have writing expertise that exceedeth that of thy students, but thou art beholden to remember that the authenticity of their experience is just as genuine as that of thine. If you are a reader who happens to be an attorney, you may be able to offer some technical or procedural nuggets to help make an attorney-character sound authentic. If you've been divorced, had skin cancer, witnessed the death of a loved one, you may be able to offer valuable suggestions to a writer working with these emotional situations. But don't preface your comments or suggestions with a special claim to authority based on your experience.

Three Tips for When Your Story is Being Discussed

Much of this advice for the writer being workshopped is implicit in the Ten Commandments For Readers. But I want to make a few points explicit:

1. Get out of your defensive crouch.
It is natural for you to think your story is the best you can write it, for you to want others to like it, and for you to be sensitive to criticism. But no matter how finished it seems, you must try to think of your story as a work-in-progress. Try this metaphor on for size: You are the sculptor of the story. As sculptor, your first order of business is a trip to the quarry. There, in a rough wall of marble, you see a rude vision of

your finished work. You direct the stonecutters to the proper location. You hire fork lift and truck. You get the piece back to your studio and up onto your work table. At this point, you have already done a heck of a lot of work. And you haven't even picked up your hammer and chisel yet. Lurking inside that hunk of stone are the lines and forms of your vision—you're thinking now it's a Madonna and child. But you still have to set about the delicate and arduous work of freeing them from the rock.

That piece of stone is your early draft. You have gone to the quarry of your experience, used the tools of your imagination to prize loose a hunk, and you've put it on the table. Now, before you have at it with a hammer, it's good for you to listen to the opinions of others. Perhaps it's not a Madonna and child, but a bust of your grandfather Ignatius. When your story is on the table, take deep breaths, open your mind and heart and imagination, and try to assimilate as much of what people say as you can. *Your business is not to defend, explain, justify, or rebut.* It is to Listen. In my workshops, the writer may ask for clarifications, but I do not allow the writer to defend, explain, justify, or rebut.[2]

2. Expect conflicting interpretations and advice.

If one reader thinks your story's too short, another probably thinks it's too long. If one thinks the story would be better without goldfish swallowing, another reader will suggest lots more goldfish, and maybe salamanders and snakes for good measure. One does not cancel out the other. It's up to the writer to take it all in, try it all on for size, attempt to see it through each reader's eyes, and then come to decisions about how to attack the rewrite.

3. Try not to maintain an over-zealous loyalty to your original vision of what the story is about.

We often reveal our true themes unintentionally, peripherally, accidentally. It's a good critic that can pick up on what's really at the heart of the story when it isn't apparent, and an even better writer who can recognize Truth in such a thing. The writer certainly should not retain undue loyalty to "what really happened." If you've used your sister's

---

2   Yes, I'm pulling rank. The Xth Commandment may be overruled for certain procedural matters.

first husband, Sid, as the model for a character, Ed, in your story, your primary concern must be Ed's action and function in this fictive world of art, and not how much or how little Ed ends up truly resembling Sid.

What is the proper response of the writer to readers who have pointed out superfluities and essentials, who have misread and correctly read, who have got right to the heart of the matter and have gone off on endless empty tangents, who have offered suggestions that make no sense and suggestions of dazzling insight?

The proper response to all the above is "Thank you."

Suggested Protocols for Effective Workshopping

These bits of advice are directed to the teacher or moderator of the workshop.

1. Circulate manuscripts in advance.
The alternatives are to waste valuable workshop time reading them privately or out loud. Although there is some advantage to hearing how a story sounds out loud, particularly in authenticity of dialogue, the advantages are outweighed by the negatives. This is a *writing* workshop, after all. A reader needs to see the work on paper, and should read it several times, in order to give his most cogent response.

2. Rotate the Moderator.
For each story being workshopped, let another student serve as moderator of the discussion. This means that each student should pay attention to the advice in this list. There's a danger here: a writer can rightly feel cheated if the discussion of her story is not skillfully moderated—and many students do not hesitate to say so. An alternative is that the teacher moderates the first round of stories in the workshop, and students moderate subsequent rounds.

3. Equal time for each story.
A writer is bound to feel cheated when the story before hers gets forty minutes of scrutiny, and there's only ten minutes left in the workshop. For the sake of democracy and good feelings, the time of the workshop should be apportioned equally to all stories, and the teacher or

moderator should stick rigorously to the schedule. This will often mean cutting short a vibrant and fruitful discussion. But so be it. The readers can engage the writer privately, later, to finish making their points. In the workshop, each story gets equal time.

Although I have previously inveighed against allowing the writer to defend, explain, justify, or rebut, I sometimes let the writer address a couple of questions to the readers, usually at a point five or ten minutes before the person's time is up.

4. Require written responses from everyone for every story.

No matter how brilliant, spoken responses vanish into the air, with only the writer's memory to preserve them. And with the deluge of information the writer has to handle, it's impossible for her to retain it all. Therefore, it's great for her to have written responses to refer to after the talking has died away and she's at home in front of her computer trying to rewrite.

Written responses are valuable for readers too, in that they force an articulation of what might otherwise remain vague feelings, and result in stammering nonsensical commentary. A reader shouldn't read aloud her response to the story, but having written it, she will be better prepared to speak extemporaneously about the work. It sometimes happens that a reader will learn more about the story through the discussion, so much so that the insights she brought to the room on paper no longer seem valid to her. In that case, I think it's a good idea for the reader to append a note to that effect to the writer, saying what changed her mind and why.

A response form can be useful to a workshop class. It imposes an expectation of length and, by having separate sections, can impose an analytical response. In my workshops, I provide a standard response form for every student for every story, sectioned according to the logic of the Parts Warehouse (Chapter 5). After a story is workshopped, the forms are handed in to me as teacher. I look them over, bundle them together with my response, and give the whole pile to the writer at the next meeting. Since part of a student's grade is based on quality response forms, students have an added incentive to do them well. A sample of the form appears at the end of this chapter.

Conclusion

A good workshop is its own reward. It is a place where trust, intimacy, and shared purpose come together to create a special kind of family, a special kind of community. Even if the writer never gets around to taking that hunk of rock to its next Updikian level of short story sophistication, the experience of talking about that thing which is so much a part of her and yet so much its own entity can be a most enlightening and satisfying episode in the ongoing story of her life.

WORKSHOP RESPONSE FORM

Title: _____

Author: _____

Reader: _____

1. Frame, Body and Drive Train
Where is the story at its best? What parts, passages, aspects show this story doing the things it does well? Give page and paragraph citations, then explain what's working well here.

_____

_____

_____

_____

2. Interiors
Give an interpretation of this story. What's the theme? What point is the story trying to make? How does it make you feel?

_____

_____

_____

_____

3. When It Goes Into The Shop
What's your advice for remaking this story? Confusions. Implausibilities. Missed Opportunities. Criticisms.

_____

_____

_____

_____

Chapter Five

The Parts Warehouse

WELCOME TO The Parts Warehouse. Any organizing metaphor for such a complex set of terminology is bound to have its problems and inconsistencies. Still, there's more logic here than in a mere alphabetical listing of terms (see the Index for that). The warehouse has four aisles:

- FRAMES & BODIES: Structural components necessary to all stories, such as point of view, tense, and narrative organization.
- ENGINES & DRIVE TRAINS: Plot and character, the things you need to make the story go.
- INTERIORS: What happens between the lines. Things like theme, tone, mood, and symbol.
- ACCESSORIES: Everything left over. Overwriting, authorial intrusion, pace, transition, and lots more.

The upper shelves of the aisles are devoted to definitions and explanations. Below them, on the lower shelf, you'll often find made-up examples or references to famous examples from literature. And every so often you'll come across a sign, like this:

which means: **WARNING: SLIPPERY FLOOR!** to alert you to common mistakes people make in this area.

The next two pages contain a more complete directory to the entire Parts Warehouse. It's self-service. Stay as long as you like, and feel free to come back for a part anytime.

Aisle A: FRAMES & BODIES

Part No.	Part Name:
A1	**POINT OF VIEW**
A1.1	1st Person
A1.2	2nd Person (⚠ gimmicky)
A1.3	3rd Person Objective
A1.4	3rd Person Limited Omniscient
A1.5	3rd Person Omniscient (⚠ shifting point of view)
A2	**TENSE**
A2.1	Simple Past
A2.2	Simple Present (⚠ mixing tenses)
A3	**STRUCTURE**
A3.1	Chronology
A3.1.1	- Linear
A3.1.2	- Non-linear, recursive
A3.1.2.1	- Flashback (⚠ overuse)
A3.1.2.2	- Frames
A3.2	Foreground
A3.2.1	- Scene
A3.2.2	- Setting
A3.3	Background
A3.3.1	- Narration
A3.3.2	- Exposition (⚠ primacy of scene)

Aisle B: ENGINES & DRIVE TRAINS

Part No.	Part Name:
B1	**PLOT**
B1.1	Standard
B1.1.1	- Rising action
B1.1.2	- Climax
B1.1.3	- Falling action
B1.2	Plot Accessories
B1.2.1	- Subplot
B1.2.2	- Foreshadowing (⚠ light touch)
B1.2.3	- *In medias res*
B1.2.4	- Obligatory scene
B1.2.5	- Epiphany
B1.2.6	- Closure
B1.2.7	- *Deus ex machina*
B2	**CHARACTER**
B2.1	Protagonist
B2.2	Narrator
B2.2.1	- Observer narrator
B2.2.2	- Unreliable narrator (⚠ planting clues)
B2.3	Antagonist
B2.4	Minor Characters
B2.4.1	- Limp
B2.4.2	- Foil
B2.5	Dialogue
B2.5.1	- Direct quotation
B2.5.2	- Indirect quotation
B2.5.3	- Dialogue tags (⚠ excess creativity)
B2.5.4	- *Non sequitur*

⚠ = Warning! Slippery Floor!

Aisle C:
INTERIORS

Part No.	Part Name:
C1	**THEMATIC ASPECTS**
C1.1	Theme
C1.2	Mood
C1.3	Tone
C1.4	Catharsis
C2	**TECHNICAL ASPECTS**
C2.1	Voice
C2.1.1	- Diction
C2.1.2	- Dialect and Accent (⚠ phony dialects)
C2.1.3	- Stream of Consciousness
C2.2	Symbol
C2.2.1	- Metaphor
C2.2.1.1	- Simile
C2.2.1.2	- Extended metaphor
C2.2.2	- Motif

Aisle D:
ACCESSORIES

Part No.	Part Name:
D1	**OVERWRITING** (⚠ over modifying)
D2	**UNDERWRITING**
D3	**PACE**
D4	**DESCRIPTION**
D4.1	Sensual showing
D4.2	Abstract telling
D4.3	Figurative comparing
D5	**TRANSITION**
D6	**AUTHORIAL INTRUSION**
D7	**ALLUSION**
D7.1	Literary & historical (⚠ plagiarism)
D7.2	Popular culture (⚠ ephemeral)
D7.3	Private (⚠ general audience)
D8	**CATEGORIES OF FICTION**
D8.1	Psychological realism
D8.2	Genre fiction (⚠ conventions)
D8.3	Minimalism
D8.4	Magical realism

⚠ **= Warning! Slippery Floor!**

Aisle A: FRAMES & BODIES

A1   POINT OF VIEW

A1.1   1st PERSON – story told by an "I" narrator. Simplest, easiest way to write a story.

> *While I was sprinkling goldfish food in the aquarium one day, it occurred to me that I didn't trust Keith.*

A1.2   2nd PERSON – a substitution for what is really a first person narrator, created by substituting "you" and "yours" for "I," "me," "mine."

> *You like goldfish. You've always liked goldfish. Sometimes you wonder about yourself; this morning, for instance, when Keith called them "conceited carp."*

⚠ Second person storytelling is a gimmicky, seldom-used convention, usually better replaced by first or third person.

A1.3   3rd PERSON OBJECTIVE – a camera-like point of view, where everything is described from the outside, the reader is permitted no access to anyone's thoughts or motivations; it's purely what happens, on the surface, as if recorded by a documentarist.

> *Beth lifted the lid of the aquarium. "Ginger, Maryanne, Skipper," she called. She sprinkled flakes from a cylindrical container.*
> *"Where's little buddy?"*

A1.4   3rd PERSON LIMITED OMNISCIENT – reader shares one character's point of view of events and actions of the narrative; reader is privileged to see that character's thoughts, but no one else's.

Keith finally decided to bring it up. "Beth," he said, "I want to talk about your goldfish."

"My goldfish?"

He saw that she wasn't going to make it easy for him. "Don't you think you spend an awful lot of time with them?"

A1.5   **3rd PERSON OMNISCIENT** – the story is related by an overarching, god-like consciousness that has the power, when it chooses, to see into any character's thoughts or motivations, can know things about characters that they themselves don't know. An omniscient narrator becomes almost an additional character in the story, a voice distinct from the voice of the characters.

For the six months that Beth had been talking to her goldfish, no one had said a thing. Her family was indulgent, her friends discreet. All of that changed when Keith entered the picture. He was the type of man who always wanted to get to the bottom of things, even if the thing happened to be a fish tank.

⚠ Students often mistake a shifting third person limited omniscience for this voice, causing problems for the narrative:

Keith finally decided to bring it up. "Beth," he said, "I want to talk about your goldfish."

Beth decided to pretend not to know what he meant. She smiled and said, "My goldfish?"

This kind of jumping back and forth between two characters' minds leaves the reader wondering whose story it is, where it's being related from.

A2   TENSE

A2.1   SIMPLE PAST TENSE – the conventional storytelling voice, sometimes called the "historical present tense" because although the verb tense is technically in the past, the reader still gets a sense of the immediacy of things occurring as they happen in the story.

Beth went down to the corner store and bought fish food.

A2.2   SIMPLE PRESENT TENSE – sometimes more effectively conveys a sense of immediacy.

Beth goes down to the corner store and buys fish food.

When using it, the writer should beware of overusing present continuous (*Beth is going down to the corner store and is buying fish food*).

⚠ Once the writer has chosen the tense of her narration, she must stick to it. One of the most common technical problems is the arbitrary mixing of tenses. One exception to this rule is that in present tense stories, flashbacks are often related in the past tense.

Beth goes [present] down to the corner store to buy fish food. She pauses [present] at the doorway and remembers [present] what happened [past] last week. Old Jack behind the counter said [past] Keith stopped [past] by, asking how much she spent on fish food.

Flashing back from a past tense story, an author will commonly use the past perfect tense, but usually only for the first couple of verbs, and then will slip back into the simple past tense for the remainder of the flashback.

A3   STRUCTURE

A3.1   CHRONOLOGY

A3.1.1   Linear – the story follows the chronological (linear) time sequence of events from the beginning of the narration to the end.

A3.1.2   Non-linear, or Recursive – the story does not follow the chronological sequence of events; instead it jumps around in some way or another.

A3.1.2.1   Flashback – the most common device for jumping around, involves removing the reader to a scene that occurred earlier, often introduced as the protagonist's memory or recollection.

⚠ 1) Flashbacks should not be over-used in a short story, or there will be too much dissonance created by all those transitions. 2) They should not be open-ended; that is, at the end of the flashback, the story should return to the time and place from before the flashback. 3) Avoid flashbacks within flashbacks.

A3.1.2.2   Framing device – the story is "framed" by an introduction and conclusion that is part of the story but in some way comments on the story as well. A once-upon-a-time bedtime story may be introduced and concluded by a grandfather sitting on the side of the bed. Famous example: *Heart of Darkness*, by Joseph Conrad, in which Marlow tells the whole story while sitting on the deck of a boat.

A3.2   FOREGROUND – the main action of the story, where the characters are moving the plot forward, increasing the tension and the reader's interest by the things they say and do. If a story's plot is based in the conflict arising from a boyfriend's jealousy of his girlfriend's attachment to her goldfish, then everything concerned with portraying that conflict and its resolution is foreground.

A3.2.1   **Scene** – the basic building block of foreground, and therefore of storymaking itself. A scene, as on stage, is the dramatic presentation of the action directly to the reader. A scene shows what the characters say and do (and sometimes what they think) in a particular time and place; it usually occurs more or less in real time.

A3.2.2   **Setting** – the locations for the foreground actions. Scenes happen in specific times and places, and the places need to be shown to the reader. Setting is not merely where the story takes place, but contributes to all other parts, especially mood, as in the famous beginning, "It was a dark and stormy night. . . ."

In Chapter 6, the story "Moving Parts" uses the auto parts counter and the tacky Holiday Inn lounge to help create the sense of the narrator's isolation and alienation; "Roots and Wings" sets its climactic scene in a root cellar, emphasizing the sad, "grounded" situation of the widow.

Extended description of setting may be considered background, but setting itself is crucial to creating the fictional foreground reality.

A3.3   **BACKGROUND** – all the supporting parts that anchor the foreground action in a believable world.

A3.3.1   **Narration** – giving a summary of what happened. Narration compresses time, leaves out detail, makes the connections and the transitions between scenes. Let's say the first scene of a story shows Keith's first visit to Beth's apartment, where she spends more time talking to her goldfish than to him. The second scene is their fight about it, which happens a week later, in a restaurant. To get from the first to the second scene, the writer might use something like this:

> *On Tuesday Keith called her at work, and invited her*
> *out to dinner that weekend. She said yes, and thanked him,*
> *but when he joked about knowing a good fish place down*
> *by the pier, she didn't laugh.*

The writer could have presented the entire phone call, with direct quotations of Beth's and Keith's dialogue, but it would have taken a lot of time and space in the story. Instead, a summation of the phone call can be presented economically in narration, and the reader is ready to move on quickly and see what happens on the date.

A3.3.2   **Exposition** – this is a broad, catch-all term whose definition overlaps with that of narration. Virtually anything that is not the foreground dramatic scenes of the story can be called exposition, whether it consists of the narrator filling in background details, explaining a situation, describing a setting or character, etc.

It is useful to note that scene and narration operate along a continuum: compress a scene enough and you can call it narration; slow down narration enough and it becomes scene. Mini-scenes can be embedded in narration or exposition (indeed, it's usually a good idea), and scenes often include bits of narration or exposition. In this excerpt from "The Elevator Man," the protagonist's expository speculation on the relative toxicity of grain dusts is illustrated by means of embedded scene (in italics):

> Tim knew milo was worst of all. He was only twelve, but he had Vaughn Jones to back him up. Vaughn had operated the grain elevator over in Talmadge for fifty-one years before he retired and moved to Julian. *Tim saw him shuffle past every day on his way to get his mail at the store, pulling that oxygen bottle on little wheels behind him. When Vaughn Jones pointed to the cloud of red dust rising up out of the back end of the truck when the milo was pouring in, shook his head and said that was the most killing grain dust there was,* you had to believe it.

The next paragraph goes back to Tim's situation. Vaughn Jones' cameo appearance is simply a part of the exposition.

⚠ While I suppose there are stories whose genius is in their exposition (the wonderful opening of J.D. Salinger's *The Catcher in the Rye* comes to mind), there's often a temptation to encumber a story with too much exposition. The fundamental challenge of storywriting is to keep the reader asking, "What happens next?" and to deliver. Beware of getting sidetracked into explanations and deliberations that hurt the pace of the story more than they contribute to its fullness.

Aisle B: ENGINES & DRIVE TRAINS

B1   PLOT

The British novelist E.M. Forster famously differentiated between plot and mere sequential occurrences: "'The king died, the queen died' is not a plot. 'The king died, the queen died *of grief*' is a plot." Forster's example refers to the *sense of causality* that is integral to plot. That is, something happens *because* the thing before it happened, and it in turn will cause something else to happen, like dominoes falling. Only imagine the dominoes becoming larger and larger until they push over a barn door.

B1.1   STANDARD PLOT COMPONENTS

B1.1.1   **Rising action** – the dominoes getting bigger, the causality becoming more complicated, the stakes climbing higher, the reader interest growing more intense. Must involve some kind of tension or conflict. Think of foreplay.

B1.1.2   **Climax** – when the tensions or conflicts at work come to a peak, a confrontation, a resolution. Think of sex.

B1.1.3   **Falling action** (denouement) – think of the cigarette.

B1.2   PLOT ACCESSORIES

B1.2.1   **Subplot** – a corollary action to the main action: King dies, queen dies of grief; court jester starts looking at the want ads.

B1.2.2   **Foreshadowing** – planting clues that prepare the reader or give hints of further complications or resolutions in plot or character.

     ▲ Foreshadowing should be lightly done; the writer usually doesn't want to tip her hand by giving away too much. Heavy-handed:

> *Little did I know this seemingly mild mannered actuary would turn out to be a swallower of goldfish!*

A lighter touch:

> *When I came into the actuary's office, I couldn't help noticing there was one less goldfish in the bowl.*

B1.2.3   *In medias res* – literally "in the middle of things," as in the way Greek epics begin. In general, it's a good idea to plop your reader right down into the middle of the action, and then try to sneak the background information in later, rather than beginning with a long preamble where you risk losing reader attention.

B1.2.4   **Obligatory scene** – generally, reader demands to witness the moment of truth, the climax, not just be told about it or that it happened, i.e. it's obligatory that the climax be shown to the reader as it happens and in detail.

B1.2.5   **Epiphany** – religious term made literary by James Joyce to describe a moment of new understanding or enlightenment in a character, often used as the climax of the story. Is often not a positive realization, as in the famous last words of Joyce's "Araby:" "Gazing up into the darkness I saw myself as a creature driven and derided by vanity; and my eyes burned with anguish and anger."

B1.2.6   Closure – whatever brings the story to a close. Writers speak of stories as having more closure (conventional climax and denouement, all strings tied up neatly) or less closure (story breaks off without resolving tensions). Less closure used to be associated with the term "slice-of-life," more recently with "minimalism." In either case, its adherents argue that it is more realistic for reflecting the raggedness and lack of closure of most real life situations. The countervailing argument is that art imposes order on the chaos of life so that resolutions are satisfying and commendable (see Chapter 2).

B1.2.7   *Deus ex machina* – literally "God out of the Machine." Refers to a sudden and highly improbable plot twist or character action which allows the plot to be resolved, e.g. the awarding of the Nobel Prize for Literature allows our destitute hero to quit wretched writing of *Fiction Workshop Companion* and devote his life to hedonism and debauchery.

B2   CHARACTER

B2.1   PROTAGONIST – the main character, usually the person upon whom the main conflict of the rising action is centered. It is possible, but uncommon, to have more than one character fulfill the protagonist function in a story.

B2.2   NARRATOR – the character who tells the story. In most first person stories, the narrator is also the protagonist. Most third person stories do not have a narrator, except in the case where a frame is created which, in a sense, turns the telling of the story over to one of the characters.

B2.2.1   **Observer narrator** – a first-person narrator who is not the protagonist. For example, the main character in F. Scott Fitzgerald's *The Great Gatsby* is Gatsby himself, but the story is related to the reader in first person by a character named Nick.

B2.2.2   **Unreliable narrator** – a narrator who, wittingly or unwittingly, does not tell the truth to the reader. In reading *Lolita*, by Vladimir Nabokov, one learns to be suspicious of Humbert Humbert's seeming ingenuousness.

⚠ If a narrator is not to be relied upon, the writer is obligated to plant clues to let the reader know this is the case. It's not fair to have the narrator turn out to be the murderer at the end of the story if nothing in the story has given the slightest clue.

B2.3   **ANTAGONIST** – "the bad guy," the character who opposes or works against the interests of the main character. A story does not need a clearly defined antagonist. The antagonist function may be spread among several characters, including the protagonist ("he was his own worst enemy"), or the function may be assumed by something non-human, such as the weather.

B2.4   **MINOR CHARACTERS** – the rest of the cast in a story. They are not unimportant; if a character has no function at all in the story, he or she should not be there.

B2.4.1   **"A Limp"** – each minor character should have some small distinguishing feature or trait.

B2.4.2   **Foil** – a character who contrasts sharply with another. One function, probably the main function, of minor characters is to set off the traits and personalities of the main characters. A generous minor character, for example, will give the writer opportunities to show facets of a major character's stinginess.

B2.5   DIALOGUE

B2.5.1   **Direct quotation** – exactly what is said, as set off by quotation marks.

"I fear the muskrat," she said.

B2.5.2   **Indirect quotation** – also known as summary dialogue or narrative dialogue, where the writer tells what the person said without quote marks.

She told him about her encounter with the muskrat.

B2.5.3   **Dialogue tags** – narrative appendages to quotes that identify the speaker. Can come before, in the middle of, or after a piece of dialogue. Most common: "said" (present tense: "says").

⚠ Beware of fancy alternatives to "said." Fat verbs such as "acknowledged," "expostulated," "exclaimed," etc. draw too much attention to themselves and, if the dialogue is good, are needlessly directive of reader interpretation (see example, page 37).

B2.5.4   *Non sequitur* – literally, "it does not follow." It's good to remember, when writing dialogue, that people don't always address the thing said immediately before, but often go back to their own concerns.

"Honey, are we all out of toilet paper again?"
"I fear the muskrat," she said.

Aisle C: INTERIORS

C1   THEMATIC ASPECTS

C1.1   THEME – what the story is about, in general, mythical, or archetypal terms. Where the story touches the deepest chords of human existence, e.g. fear of growing old, spousal jealousy, what constitutes success or fulfillment, parent-child freedom versus control, coping with grief, etc.

C1.2   MOOD – the emotional ambience that the story creates. Somber, playful, pensive. It can change over the course of a story. "Moving Parts" (in Chapter 6) maintains its matter-of-fact tone, but the mood changes from light-hearted to sad as the story progresses.

C1.3   TONE – refers to the author's attitude toward the story, closely related to the term "distance," referring to how close the author is to her characters or story. Tone may be passionate, involved, close, or distant, clinical, detached. It can be ironic, dead-pan, sarcastic, earnest, glib, awestruck, reverential, matter-of-fact.

C1.4   CATHARSIS – a term applied by Aristotle to Greek tragedy, it's the sudden powerful purging of emotions that the reader undergoes through the experience of the story; simply put, it's what jerks the tears in a tearjerker. At the end of John Steinbeck's *Of Mice and Men*, when the reader is a puddle of prodigious weeping because George has just shot Lenny in the head, that's catharsis.

C2   TECHNICAL ASPECTS

C2.1   VOICE – a style or attitude or mannerisms that pervade the storytelling, in any point of view. The story's voice is that from which the reader derives her sense of the story's mood and tone. It's what gives the story its distinctive idiosyncratic identity.

C2.1.1   **Diction** – word choice (not pronunciation), the single most important contribution to voice.

They contemplated the panoply of beverages in the armoire.

They checked out the stuff to drink in the cupboard.

Although the sense is the same in these two examples, the diction suggests quite different pictures of who "they" are, and the kind of party they're attending.

C2.1.2   **Dialect and Accent** – imitating the style or speech patterns of a particular region or group using phonetic spellings, altered word order and rhythms.

⚠ Dialects and accents are more difficult than they appear. Generally, a writer shouldn't try it unless she is very familiar with the dialect or accent she wants the reader to hear; sprinkling in a lot of "bloody's" and "jolly good's" does not a British accent make. A writer must be especially wary of ethnic stereotyping; a poor attempt to imitate an African American dialect can sho 'nuff create the impression of racism even though that is not at all the writer's intent. Also, there's no point in studding conversation with lots of "Uh's" and "Um's" and "Er's." Yes, it's realistic, but it, uh, also gets, um, you know, real annoying, uh, real quick.

C2.1.3   **Stream of Consciousness** – an attempt by the writer to directly convey the thoughts of a character as they occur, without explanations; often done with syntactical or grammatical innovation. Technique often associated with Virginia Woolf and James Joyce, but can be traced to the earliest novels, e.g. *Tristram Shandy*, by Laurence Sterne.

"By the End of February," in Chapter 6, is an example of this technique being employed in diary entries.

C2.2   SYMBOL – something that represents something else in a story. A concrete thing can be a symbol of something abstract, e.g. if a male character takes great pride in his necktie, the necktie may represent his vanity, or more specifically his sense of his virility (phallic symbol).

Sam always wore his most garish pink and purple tie on first dates; if the woman said she liked it, he took it as a sign that she might be open to the idea of physical intimacy.

C2.2.1   Metaphor – a more explicit symbolization, equating one thing with another. Metaphorical language can be done with nouns, verbs, or more complex syntaxes.

A fine short story is a diamond.

C2.2.1.1   Simile – a specific kind of metaphor, one that uses "like" or "as" in the comparison.

A fine short story is like a diamond.

C2.2.1.2   **Extended metaphor**, also known as a Conceit – a metaphor in which the multiple attributes or perspectives of the symbolic relationship are explored at some length.

The swamp of personal experience dries out, gets covered up, and with the passage of time becomes the coal of memory. The writer locates that coal, compresses it mightily with thought and sensibility, excavates it onto paper, cuts and polishes it with technical expertise, and—if she is lucky—eventually is in possession of the shining diamond of a short story.

C2.2.2   Motif – images or techniques or symbols that pop up more than once in a story, adding to its sense of internal unity and logic. In "By the End of February" (Chapter 6), the diarist narrator pops up with seemingly random, seemingly off-the-wall, "story ideas." But to the attentive reader, these nuggets form a commentary on the foreground action of the story. One might refer to the "story idea" motif.

Aisle D: ACCESSORIES

D1   OVERWRITING

Telling the reader too much, or too dramatically.

⚠ Although there are certain circumstances where overwriting is warranted—mainly to achieve comic effect—it is almost always a fault. The reader feels the writer is intrusive, an overbearing presence. Overwriting can slow down a story, can make the reader want to tell the writer to get out of the way and let the story tell itself. Occurs when writer interprets too much for the reader, tells reader what she already knows, or employs too many modifiers:

> *Ten year old red-headed left-handed Josh McCain used his often dirty left hand, since he was left-handed, to pull a gross, slimy, long, thin, brown earthworm out of the left front pocket of his faded but not perforated with holes Levi 501 blue jeans for boys.*

In describing emotional situations, overwriting leads to problems of sentimentality and/or melodrama:

> *Mrs. McCain cruelly smashed Josh, her own flesh and blood, with her hard vicious fist, even though the poor defenseless boy was only ten and couldn't be expected to know that his mother hated the very sight of gross slimy earthworms!*

D2   UNDERWRITING

Generally a good thing, providing more space for the reader's imagination to fill in gaps and details. As a general rule, the more intrinsically emotional the subject matter (e.g. death of a loved one), the more underwritten, spare, lean, should be the writing. The subject carries its own emotional wallop, the writer doesn't have to resort to verbal fireworks to get it across. Underwriting can be an effective technique to convey the simplicity of a child's point of view, as in "Pooh," or to create a world of unspoken tension, as in "Hollow" (both stories are in Chapter 6).

D3   PACE

The speed at which the story seems to move. Should be appropriate to the style and content of the story. Longer, more complicated sentences tend to slow pace and create a more reflective, meditative effect.

In the bath tub, when the water had turned tepid and the entire house was still, Beth liked to imagine her goldfish in the water with her, playful, as if she were swimming with the dolphins at Ocean World. In such moments, it seemed as if Keith and his insane jealousy existed on some distant dry planet, a landscape of rocks and dust, desert and dry mountain ranges.

An action passage should be fast paced. Short, declarative sentences with active verbs convey a sense of speed.

Beth burst through the door. Keith looked up, smiled evilly, and pulled the Drano from his trench coat. "No," she screamed, and threw herself across the room. His fingers stumbled on the child-proof cap, and she knocked him backward. The bottle flew out of his hand. But his flailing arm caught the corner of the fish tank. It toppled slowly forward and burst like a forty-gallon bomb, sending Ginger,

*the Professor, and Maryanne skittering across the carpet to
her feet.*

D4   DESCRIPTION

An indispensable accessory in the relation of Setting, Plot,
Character, Foreground and Background.

D4.1   **SENSUAL SHOWING** – often referred to as "concrete"
description; the most compelling and useful descriptions
create images that appeal directly to the senses, especially
sight. The more specific the details, the more appeals to the
various senses, the better.

> *Keith's new sunglasses were aviator-style. The large,
> mirror-shade lenses hung down almost to his mustache.*

D4.2   **ABSTRACT TELLING** – sometimes it is useful to describe
an effect, or summarize a moment or an emotion for the
reader.

> *Keith didn't think he looked silly. He had already
> decided that the new glasses made him handsome and
> mysterious.*

D4.3   **FIGURATIVE COMPARING** – refers to the creation of
metaphor, simile and symbol in describing things.

> *Keith's mirror shades gave him insect eyes; he looked
> like a praying mantis with a mustache.*

D5   TRANSITION

Any word, phrase, sentence or paragraph that provides a
bridge from one section of a story to another, between
scenes, in and out of flashbacks, etc.

D6 AUTHORIAL INTRUSION/ SELF-CONSCIOUSNESS

A technique associated with post-modernism, although it has been present since the dawn of fiction. It's when the story or a character somehow acknowledges the artificiality of the work. It's like an aside in a play, where a character turns and speaks directly to the audience.

D7 ALLUSION

Reference within the story to something the writer expects the reader to know.

D7.1 **LITERARY and HISTORICAL** – by direct quote or reference, bringing the force of famous words or situations to bear in a story.

When Keith opened the door and saw all of Beth's friends, with their goldfish pendants and their goldfish earrings, he knew it wasn't the "little party" she had promised. It was the Alamo.

⚠ Literary allusions, if too obscure, run the risk of crossing a line into the crime of plagiarism. If a character is contemplating suicide, the writer can have her say, "To be or not to be is indeed the question here," and the reader can be expected to get the Hamlet reference. But if a depressed and cynical character says, "Point me out the happy man and I will point you out either extreme egotism, evil—or else an absolute ignorance," the writer is obligated to make sure the reader knows that the original speaker of that line was a policeman named Scobie in Graham Greene's *The Heart of the Matter*.

D7.2 **POPULAR CULTURE** – movies, television shows, songs, commercials, pop culture mythologies (Elvis lives!), can be a rich source of allusive material for stories.

⚠ The popular culture memory is notoriously short term. When the source passes out of popular lore, these allusions can be confusing, or can make a story seem dated. "Where's the beef?" an advertising slogan that gained some prominence by being borrowed in the 1988 political campaigns, has pretty much vanished.

D7.3   PRIVATE – It can be fun to make private allusions that only specific readers will get, e.g. to the plot or characters of another story that's been workshopped in your writers group.

⚠ Obviously, a writer should not put private allusions into a story that she intends or hopes will at some point be read by strangers. For all allusions, a good rule of thumb is that it should add to the story if the reader gets it, but should not detract or confuse if the reader doesn't get it.

D8   CATEGORIES OF FICTION

D8.1   PSYCHOLOGICAL REALISM – An umbrella term for stories about real people, their lives and conflicts and concerns and tragedies, the kind of storymaking this book discusses.

D8.2   GENRE FICTION – Stories that adhere to certain accepted formulas or norms, such as romance, crime, western, war, action, thriller, science fiction, fantasy.

⚠ A common mistake is to presume that these genres are easier to write and/or are intrinsically more interesting than psychological realism. To write genre fiction, one must not only be thoroughly acquainted with the conventions of the specific genre, but one must also have a good working knowledge of most of the other terms and concepts in the Parts Warehouse.

D8.3   MINIMALISM – An approach to writing which professes that fiction should reflect the chaos of life rather than impose order onto it. Tends to reject the traditional plot sequence of rising action, climax and denouement in favor of a storyline that goes along for a while and then just stops, savoring the smallest nuances of realistic human behavior along the way. Can leave non-minimalist reader feeling cheated. Often associated with *New Yorker* magazine; in earlier era sometimes referred to as "slice-of-life" story. See "Hollow" in Chapter 6.

D8.4   MAGICAL REALISM – A term applied to a style of writing where seemingly impossible things occur in otherwise realistic narrations. An angel speaks to a character, for example. Associated with South American writers.

Chapter Six

Stories

ROOTS AND WINGS

by Janet Mast

THE ENTIRE FAMILY agreed that the unfortunate peckerhead incident marked the emergence of "mother's problem." In sixty-five years, no one could remember hearing Miriam Morgan swear. Not even "damn!" under her breath when she stubbed her toe for the hundredth time on her husband's bowling ball which he always left just inside the porch door although the closet was less than twelve inches away. When a woman raises four children and is never heard describing them in terms stronger than "spirited," such restraint does not go unnoticed. In Franconia, Miriam was known as a woman of refinement.

So when Miriam, while passing the candied yams around a crowded Thanksgiving table, referred to her late husband, Franklin, as "that peckerhead sonofabitch" there was instant rapt silence.

Carol was not there when it happened. She was sleeping off the flu in her apartment, but she heard about it soon after in the flurry of phone calls from concerned relatives.

"Spellbound. I would say we were spellbound," said her brother Wesley, calling from Pheasterville early next morning. His voice had a tendency to crack when he got ex-

> *From*
> *The Parts Warehouse:*
> *In this story, note how the author employs foreshadowing, flashback, symbol, and setting.*

cited. "Mom just sat there, holding the yams out. 'Course, Uncle Bud was too dumbfounded to take them so she just set them down and started to eat!"

After the call, Carol swallowed a couple of Tylenol, anticipating the high-pitched frenzy of her sister-in-law, Luanne. Somehow she knew it would be Luanne, not Mason, who would call. Her middle brother was not much for talking. He was uncomfortable with displays of emotion, but Luanne more than made up for it.

"In front of the *kids* too! Mason and I were *disgusted!* You should be *thankful* you weren't there to see it!" Carol held the phone slightly away from her ear to give the Tylenol a fighting chance. She could still hear every word. "My *Stewart* has never heard such language, I can tell you that! And about his own dead *grandfather*! It makes you want to cry!"

By noon, Carol was on her third cup of tea and actually looking forward to Frank's sardonic comments. He was the oldest. "Most of the kids looked real impressed. Especially young Stewart. He was the only one with voice enough to say anything out loud," said Frank.

"What did he say?" asked Carol, imagining the ten-year-old's face alight with admiration.

"He said, 'Geeze Louise, Gramma!'"

Carol hung up after Frank's customary "So long kid," and tried to sort out the pieces of what she had heard. Miriam's sensational comment at the table was bizarre, but her "problem" had a more troubling aspect. After dinner, she had packed two suitcases and left for the mountain cabin in Wellsboro, offering no explanation beyond, "I'm going to the cabin for a while. The mountains are beautiful this time of year." The opinion held by the family till then was that Miriam had never much liked the mountains.

The three brothers held an emergency caucus and elected Carol, in absentia, to "speak to Mother." They felt she was best equipped for the job by reason of gender. She hesitated for two days, vacillating. Carol was reserved by nature and found few things more unpleasant than intrusiveness. Her mother's desire for privacy seemed implicit. Still, Saturday noon found Carol throwing an overnight bag, a thermos of coffee and Rand McNally into the front seat of her Honda. Driven by honorable concern and base curiosity, she headed northwest.

The day had started out cloudy, but by late afternoon the sun was squinting through the trees lining the narrow Allegheny roads. Their branches reached out for each other, entwining overhead. Gaudy colored leaves rained down, swirling in the wake of the tires. Carol tried to concentrate on driving. She hadn't been to the cabin in almost fifteen years. These rambling mountain roads and their scattered farmhouses all looked alike. She liked knowing where she was at all times, she always had. Thirty-four now, she could still remember the sickening feeling of uncertainty she'd felt as a child as soon as the scenery became unfamiliar.

"Daddy, are we lost?" she would ask.

"Well now that you mention it, yes Carol, we are lost. In fact I don't think we've ever been this lost. The next town we come to, I'm going to stop and buy a house, because I don't think we'll ever find our old one. Too bad. It was a nice house."

Carol knew he was teasing, but her stomach knotted up anyway and only the sound of her brothers laughing at her from the back of the station wagon kept the tears back.

"Listen honey," her father said. "There are worse things than not knowing where you are." Even then, Carol knew her father believed this to be true.

It was dusk when Carl reached the cabin. It looked like a child left too long without its mother, dirty-faced and ragged. Her father told everyone that his cabin was "maintenance free" but like anything of value, in reality it was not. Over the years the cedar siding had faded to grey. But Carol remembered it a warm brown and her first impression was one of decay, as though the house had died along with its owner. One of the shutters had worked loose from the hinge and hung askew. All the shutters needed paint, but the windows they framed were bright. As the car ground along the rutted driveway, Carol could see her mother standing in the doorway.

Miriam did not come out, but watched Carol from behind the screen door. Her face was in shadow, but her form was limned in light from inside the house.

There was something about her mother that felt vaguely wrong to Carol as she approached, and she realized it was the stillness. Miriam was standing perfectly still. Carol was accustomed to Miriam in motion. When receiving visitors she would meet them on the porch and escort them into her home in the gathering darkness.

"Hello, Mom. How are you?" And what, precisely, are you doing up here?

"I'm fine. I'm glad you're here." Miriam swung open the door and stepped back to allow her daughter to enter. Carol carried two shopping bags full of groceries so their hug was awkward. They both spoke at once:

"I brought a few things," from Carol.

"You didn't need to bring anything," from her mother. Miriam took one of the bags.

"Let's put these in the kitchen and say hello properly. What is all of this anyway?"

"I thought I would make supper for us tonight and while I was in the grocery store I remembered that useless little market up here where we always shopped, so I picked up a few extras."

"Tiger's Filling Station and Grocery? I guess you remembered what your dad always said about Tiger's."

"'If they've got it at Tiger's, you probably don't need it.' I remember."

They deposited the bags on the counter in the tiny kitchen, and faced each other.

"Tiger's was torn down about five years ago. There's a Safeway now. You can get anything."

Carol laughed and said, "Things change, don't they."

The daughter looked at her mother's face and found it beautiful, as always. She had soft white hair that waved back from her face, combed into a loose bun. Her eyes were either grey or blue, Carol could never decide. Now they were watchful. Waiting. Her eyes set her apart from the rest of the family. The four children had dark brown eyes, like their father. Miriam was a small woman. A small woman among tall men, was how Carol thought of her. Carol was tall too. Having her mother look up at her made her want to sit down.

"The boys sent you to check up on me," said Miriam.

"They're worried about you up here alone. So am I."

"You must be hungry." Miriam turned away and began unpacking the groceries. Carol moved to help her and silence stretched between them. It was not uncomfortable. There was something comforting about this kind of work. Two women in a kitchen, putting things in their places and preparing a meal, practical activities requiring few words. They were in familiar waters, more easily navigated than the conversation they were retreating from. Carol made spaghetti. Miriam made salad. Carol had brought a loaf of crusty Italian bread and a cheap bottle of red wine. They sat down at the table. While they ate, they talked about Carol's work. She worked in an electronics lab, making liquid crystal digital displays for cars. Monotonous work, good pay. They talked about Mason, Wesley and Frank. Their marriages. Their children. They talked about the cabin. About Carol's father. How it didn't seem possible he'd been dead two years already. About Phillip, the man Carol was dating.

"No," Carol said. "We're not what you'd call serious."

Phillip had told her recently that he loved her. Carol was thinking of ways to end the relationship. She had ventured into love before and found it scary, vague territory. She preferred the familiar ground of friendship.

After two hours of talk, the bottle was empty, Carol's tongue felt furry and her lips were numb. She guessed she had finished most of it herself. Odd, because she really didn't like wine. In the bathroom she splashed cold water on her face and peered critically at her reflection in the mirror. She was never completely at peace with her face. She thought her features were too regular, pleasant but uninteresting. She'd always wished for a Streisand nose. Her best friend in high school had one blue eye and one brown eye and Carol had thought this exotic and enviable. She didn't even have the distinction, like her brothers, of prematurely grey hair. Carol shook her head slightly, to clear her mind of such meritless thoughts. She reminded herself that she was too old to obsess over her appearance in bathrooms.

When Carol returned to the kitchen, the table was cleared and her mother was gone. Carol checked the bedrooms and found them empty. She was standing in the living room, wondering if Miriam had run away again, when she noticed the light under the basement door. The basement steps were dusty and the air was damp and cool. It was a large basement, crowded with relics of abandoned childhood. Bikes and sleds, fishing rods and baseball bats leaned against each other in idle disarray. Her father's workbench stood against one wall, cluttered with tools and oil-stained cardboard boxes. He needed it, he had said, for repairs on the boys' collection of dirtbikes and snowmobiles. This room belonged to the men in the family. Miriam was sitting on a dirty wooden chair near a pile of large, half inflated black inner tubes, crying.

"I came down for a light bulb. The light in the kitchen burned out." Miriam spoke without looking up. "Just look at this junk. What am I supposed to do with all this?" Carol had never seen her mother cry. She tried to approach, but when Miriam spoke again, the strange strangled sound of her voice held Carol motionless.

"There was never a man so given to collecting junk. He was a packrat and this basement was his burrow. I kept order everywhere else, and no matter how he teased, he liked it that way. He needed it. I know you kids loved him best for his crazy ways. You saw me as some kind of a drone, trudging along behind him. I wasn't exciting or dangerous. I knew that. But I never minded because if I hadn't been there, he couldn't have done it. I was necessary. I gave him the power. You didn't know it, but he did. He talked about it. Roots and wings, he said. I would give him roots, take care of him, keep him from losing himself in his dreams. And he was supposed to give me wings. Keep me from drowning in tidiness and order. Christ, that man could talk! I was his ballast, he said. His touchstone. He could go off flying in all directions because I was there to keep things in order! That was the deal, you know. We had a deal, Goddamn him! We had a deal!"

Miriam's voice bounced off musty concrete and Carol cringed at the alien fury. Her mother's body, which had been rigid through her outburst, suddenly sagged in the old chair. She covered her face with her hands.

Carol found her feet and moved to Miriam's side. Kneeling on the cold floor she rested her head on her mother's lap.

"Mama, do you remember those tubes?"

Miriam didn't answer. In the silence, Carol remembered.

It had been raining for three days at the cabin. Carol was eleven years old. The rain didn't bother her because she was lost in *The Secret Garden*, but her brothers were liked caged leopards, pacing and snarling. They had long since exhausted their supply of indoor games and were beginning to turn on each other. Their mother, who viewed the rain as an opportunity to wage war on hidden dirt, was cleaning everything that didn't move. She interrupted her labors periodically to oversee the escalating war between her sons. The father surveyed the group from the couch. When tensions mounted to the point where bloodshed seemed imminent, he stood, disappeared into the basement and emerged moments later.

"Put on your rain gear. We're moving out. Carol and Miriam, you too." No one argued, but Miriam would not leave until she finished wiping off cans and replacing them in the pantry.

"I will not leave a job half-finished," she said. No one argued with Miriam, either.

Quarters were tight in the station wagon due to the presence of six large, black inner tubes in the back. The father responded to the barrage of questions about their destination with a cryptic "you'll see."

He drove through the fog, higher up the mountain and parked on the shoulder of the road, unloaded the inner tubes and stacked them next to the car. It was still raining but the trees provided some shelter and the family stood under dripping leaves looking down a steep embankment. At the bottom of the incline was meadow, blanketed in mist. The father picked up an inner tube and walked several feet until he came to a break in the treeline. A narrow path snaked downwards to the meadow. He placed his tube in the ground and sat in it. He looked at his family and said, "The trick is not to oversteer." Then he pushed off, hard, with his feet and careened wildly down the slope. The tube picked up speed and began to rotate, narrowly missing trees and rocks, finally sliding to a halt in the tall grass.

Mason, Wesley and Frank Jr. scrambled for their inner tubes and followed their father, rebel yells echoing down the mountain.

"C'mon Carol! Don't be a puss!" Wes hollered from the bottom.

Their father shouted, "How 'bout it Mim? A little mud won't hurt you!"

Miriam stood under her umbrella and answered with measured dignity. "Franklin, you may risk life and limb if you choose. I will wait in the car." She turned to Carol. "Do you want to do this, Carol?"

Carol looked down the incline and imagined the dizzying feeling of sliding crazily over wet leaves and mud, out of control. She knew that Wes would call her a puss, but her fear of that wild ride was greater than her fear of ridicule. She said, "No." Mother and daughter stayed in the car. Father and sons tubed for the remainder of the afternoon and most of the next day.

Twenty-five years later in a dusty basement, Carol put her arms around her mother and led her up the stairs into her bedroom. Miriam seemed smaller than usual. Tired and frail. She did not protest when Carol helped her undress for bed. Her cheek when Carol kissed it felt dry. "I love you," Carol whispered. "Don't be afraid." She didn't know if her mother heard her.

The bed she slept in was the same one she had slept in as a child. She dreamed of her father, flying, while a small girl ran below him. When she woke the dream faded from her mind, dissipating like smoke when she reached for it. She dressed quietly in the grey light while Miriam slept. Carol's thoughts wandered, and she made no attempt to control the direction her mind was taking. Her mother's door was slightly open and she thought briefly about going to wake her. Instead, she left a note about needing to get home and calling her later. Then she went down to the basement and sat in the chair where her mother had cried. She tried to think why she had come down, and there seemed to be no reason for it. She could think of no reason for picking up one of the dusty inner tubes either, but she did. Moments later she was leaving the cabin, closing the screen door quietly behind her. She tossed the tube in the back of her car and sat without moving for what seemed like a long time. As she put the car in gear, she glanced back at the house. Miriam stood in her nightgown at the door. Her hand was raised, palm outward, a gesture either a wave or a salute.

Comment

The first sentence of this story is a gem, serving simultaneously to hook the reader's interest and to **foreshadow** the conflict that animates the story. Except for one word, the sentence bespeaks the gravity of the family situation denoted delicately as "mother's problem." But no matter how it is bracketed, held in tongs by the starchy terms "unfortunate" and "incident," the silly, lewd word "peckerhead" slices through the formality and renders the situation somehow ridiculous.

The story effectively employs two **flashbacks** to give the reader glimpses of the flighty, engaging nature of Miriam's late husband, Franklin. The climax of the story reveals that "mother's problem" is nothing more, but nothing less than her grief over Franklin's death. Notice that in putting Miriam's climactic outburst in a dim musty basement, the author is slyly employing **setting** to confirm that without her husband's "wings," there is something empty and dark in Miriam's sense of order and propriety, her "roots."

These **symbols** of the complementary relationship in the marriage of Miriam and Franklin are nicely mediated in the protagonist, Carol. At the end of the story, the reader is unsure whether she will carry the inner tube to the hill to re-enact her father's flight, or merely pack it away for sentiment, an ambivalence that is echoed in the mother's gesture, which was "either a wave or a salute."

MOVING PARTS

by Joe Roberts

A FTER I GOT OUT of high school I worked at a local auto parts store. The automotive aftermarket had not been my life's ambition, but I needed a job. A month had passed since graduation and my father was getting tired of finding me on the couch every afternoon when he came home from work. The ultimatum was given: I either found a job within the next six weeks or I could follow my two older brothers into the military. Knowing that my sensibilities could not handle performing bodily functions in the presence of strangers, I decided to check the want ads.

I spent the entire week before the summer solstice rising early every morning in an attempt to get the jump on all the other young inexperienced job seekers. I could only conclude that my competition had connections with the newspaper typesetters, for by 9:00 every potential employer I called had already filled the position, thank you. This scene repeated itself until I found an ad that read: "Stockperson wanted. No Exp. Nec. Call Bill." Having as little Exp. as possible I called Bill and set up an interview. As the appointed time approached I walked to the address Bill had given me.

*From
The Parts
Warehouse:
In this story,
watch for Roberts'
effective use of
indirect dialogue,
non sequitur,
"limps" and
falling action.*

This would be the first job that I would ever have and the prospect of so much responsibility, any responsibility, made me nervous. I walked past the store. I walked back. I stood outside. I feigned interest in a display of oil cans in the window. When the store seemed sufficiently emptied of customers I went inside.

I walked to the counter. A fat young man with a Quaker State cap on his head and the name "Jerry" stitched to his torn pocket asked if he could help me. I told him I was there about the job.

"What job? A blow job?"

"Uh, no. The one in the paper for a stockperson, no experience necessary, call Bill?"

He punched the intercom and tossed me a form which I was to fill out while the owner, a Mr. William Wersler, finished a phone call. Having no previous employment, I didn't take long in filling out the form. I checked and rechecked my answers while Jerry made up new lyrics for the Eagles tape in the stereo.

"There's gonna be a hard-on tonight, a hard-on tonight, I know."

Just as I was losing courage from staring at the blank spaces on the form, a tall, grayhaired man came out and put out his hand. "Hi, I'm Bill Wersler," he said.

I told him my name and he told me what the job involved (more than I knew) and what it paid (less than I had hoped) and asked if I knew how to drive.

"Yes," I said, "but no stick."

"No shit," he replied.

He said the choice was narrowed down to me and some other guy and that he'd call later that day.

I walked home, carefully slipped the tie over my head to preserve the knot, and made lunch. I was eating an untoasted Pop-Tart when the phone rang. It was Mr. Wersler asking if I could start that afternoon.

An hour later I was back at the store unpacking air filters, stocking electrical parts and filling orders for exhaust pipes. At five-thirty the store closed, and Mr. Wersler asked me if I had memorized the entire inventory yet. He was joking, but I reminded myself that I could always quit. Anyway, I had a job. I had something to tell people when they asked me what I did.

After a couple of weeks I got acclimated to the job but I never felt part of the camaraderie of Jerry and the other countermen. I didn't know anything about setting the timing chain on a '78 Firebird and I couldn't settle debates about carburetor adjustments on K-cars. I tried to compensate by being as conscientious as possible, but it didn't make me one of the guys. My suspicion that women were human beings too made it difficult for me to appreciate the Rigid Tool Calendar hanging by the loading dock door. This calendar of scantily clad women was so named not for its effect upon the looker, but for the brand name of the tools the women were suggestively holding. My co-workers sensed my uneasiness with the pictures and teased me.

One day I got diarrhea from having a quart of Hershey's chocolate milk for lunch. When I finally came out of the bathroom Jerry asked me what I had been doing in there for so long.

"What do you think?" I asked, trying to sound casual.

"I think you were taming the snake," he said and made a stroking motion towards his crotch.

Another time Jerry sprayed starting fluid through the keyhole of the bathroom when I was inside. When I was waiting on customers he'd duck down behind the counter, make farting noises with his armpit and proclaim loudly, "Jesus Christ! Something died!"

One of the benefits of having a steady job was having a disposable income. To dispose of it I began spending my nights at the Captain's Lounge of the Holiday Inn off of Route 100. In addition to the leather-look vinyl captains' chairs and barmaids in fish net stockings, this place featured live bands with names like "Cherri and the Big Popper" and "Norman's Mother."

The Saturday after the Fourth of July, when "Mother" was finishing up their holiday engagement, I met a young woman who had just broken up with her boyfriend. I asked her to dance. I bought us some drinks. She told me her boyfriend was such a bastard. I told her I worked for an auto parts store. She told me how the bastard had run off with her car, but first he did teach her lots of useful stuff like uncorroding battery terminals with club soda. I said I liked it with white wine and ordered another round. We danced until closing. I walked her outside to her van. She said I was a nice guy. She opened the door, got in and drove away. A week later I ran into her at a gas station. She and the bastard had reconciled and were getting married.

When I wasn't not going home with women I was usually getting cornered by drunken strangers who wanted to tell me their troubles. The band would play loudly and I couldn't hear what the drunks were saying, but I'd just nod my head and be their best buddy. One night I met a father and son from North Carolina who were working at a nearby power plant. They picked up my tab for the whole evening because I had been gracious enough to share my table with them. The son noticed the way I always put my sports coat on before I asked a woman to dance. The father said this was the mark of a gentleman. I didn't bother to tell him it was where I kept my wallet.

Another night I met the girl who had been the prom date of my best friend. The friend had subsequently dropped out of school and, I am told, is now living in a home for the mentally unstable. Whatever the case, I found his prom date, Pam, dateless on this evening. Back in school, she was quiet, chubby, and not very pretty. Her one fashion move was to dye her hair a shade of blond that was too light for her complexion. In the months since I'd last seen her, however, she'd lost weight, let her natural color grow out, and cut her hair in a smart new style. I was flattered the way she hugged me and chatted as if we'd been best friends in school. She wore a tight top, and I found her fleshiness enticing.

"Do you have any pictures from the prom?" she asked.

"No, Donna has them all."

"Oh. Do you still go with her?"

"No. She threw me over for some older guy with a poodle and a motorboat."

"Gee, that's too bad." But she said it with a grin.

Pam and I had fun reliving high school memories. We were midway through junior year when I noticed a bald guy leering at me from the doorway. It was Jerry without his Quaker State cap. This was the first time I had seen him outside of the store. He kept smiling at me as he motioned to someone. I cringed at the thought that he and some other guys from work might be out on the town and decide to embarrass me in front of Pam.

As I was thinking of some way to excuse myself and perhaps head Jerry off at the door, a buxom Italian-looking woman took his arm. He led her to where Pam and I were sitting.

"Hi, mind if we join yuhz?" he asked.

"Be our guests," I said.

He turned to the woman and said "Honey, this is the guy at work I was telling you about."

I wondered what he had told her about me. Did this woman know about Jerry's goosing me with an oil can funnel and giving me a wedgie with a vice grips? Would he recount it for Pam's benefit?

Jerry grinned and said, "This is my wife, Linda."

Linda and I said "hello" and I introduced Pam.

"Tonight's our anniversary," Jerry said. "Five years."

I congratulated them and Jerry ordered drinks. It turned out that Pam and Linda both worked for the same knitting mill on different shifts. They talked about piece work rates, and I was left to talk about the store with Jerry. The waitress who served drinks was wearing a mini tuxedo outfit and Jerry made a remark about nice tails. Linda shot him a look and Jerry looked sheepish. I'd never seen him look that way before. It got late and Linda had to work a double shift the next day so she and Jerry excused themselves.

The following Monday Jerry told the guys at the store that he had seen me with a good-looking babe at the Holiday Inn. One of them asked if we had gotten a room with a vibrating bed.

"I bet they made their own vibrations," Jerry said.

I smiled.

Three weeks later our store was short on an order of exhaust pipes from the warehouse so Jerry and I took the van to pick up the difference. Halfway down route 30, Jerry made a u-turn across the median strip and pulled into a Roy Rogers for lunch.

It was two o'clock so there was no one near our booth by the fixins bar. Jerry said he liked the food better here than at Burger King even though Roy was more expensive.

"Do you still go out with Pam?" he asked.

"We're not actually going out," I explained. "We just ran into each other that night. I'm going to call her, though. She's nice."

Jerry nodded.

"Do you and Linda go out a lot?" I asked.

"No, she doesn't like to that much. She only agreed to it that night because it was our anniversary."

He looked down at his burger, then met my eyes. "We've separated," he said.

"Oh," I said, with as little inflection as I could.

"It's not what I want," he continued. "She wants it."

"Did she say why?"

"I don't know. She won't say anything specific. Lately she finds fault with everything I do. You know, when we first started dating, before we got married, she kept a diary of every time we had sex. I seen it. Once we even did it on a clothes dryer."

This time Jerry was not talking about sex to embarrass me, but I still felt at a loss for words. He looked at me.

"I'm flattered that you would confide in me," I said.

"You're the only guy from work I ever introduced to Linda. She said she thought you were nice."

We talked some more and, unable to think of anything else, I suggested marriage counseling.

After that day Jerry stopped goosing me with gear shifts. He tried the old jokes, but it seemed like he couldn't pull it off. When no one else was around, he asked my advice about women. As if I knew. I called Pam a couple of times, and we had fairly long talks on the phone. She was working second shift, so we had a hard time trying to find a time to get together. But she always sounded happy to hear from me. Call back any time, she said.

A week before Labor Day an opening came up at the warehouse. Jerry put in for it and got it. About that time I realized that I didn't want to spend my life unpacking alternators so I enrolled in a night course at the community college. Then I took a weekend job at Pizza Hut, closing cook for Friday and Saturday nights. I had to stay until two or three o'clock in the morning scouring the burnt ziti from the pasta dishes. My hands would smell like pepperoni for three days. This routine plus my school work left me little time to go out. I looked forward to the semester break at Christmas when I could invite Pam for a real date.

The second week of December an electrical problem closed the Pizza Hut early, so I dropped by the Holiday Inn. I thought of things I could tell Pam, like it's strange how such a tacky place could feel like home. I walked through the lobby, imagining how I'd make fun of the twin aluminum trees with the red satin balls and twinkling pink lights. Along the entrance to the Captain's Lounge plastic boughs of holly were strung among the fish nets. Pam would appreciate that.

I sat at the bar. The bartender remembered me and asked where I'd been hiding. As he poured me a glass of Riunite Red on the rocks I scanned the room for other familiar faces. In a booth at the far end of the room I saw Jerry. He saw me and smiled back. He was holding hands across the table with a dark-haired woman, and I felt good for him. I wondered if he had taken my suggestion of marriage counseling. It had just been a stab in the dark on my part, but maybe Jerry was capable of making a sincere effort to save his marriage.

When the band took a break I walked over to talk to Jerry and Linda. As I stepped around the Christmas tree I saw that the woman in the booth was Pam. There was a silence, in which I watched Pam's hand slowly withdraw to her own side of the table.

"Hi Jerry," I said. "Pam."

They each smiled.

"How's things down at the store?" Jerry said. "Never see youse anymore."

I told him about college and Pizza Hut and shifted my eyes between the two of them.

"That's nice," Pam said, still smiling.

"How are things at the mill?" I asked.

"I don't work there anymore. Jerry got me a job at the warehouse," she said.

"Oh."

There was another silence and we all continued to smile.

"Well," I said, "I only stopped in for a quick drink. I was invited to a Christmas party at the house of one of the girls I go to school with. Guess I'll head over there. Nice seeing both of you."

"Nice seeing you," they said.

As I walked back to my car I saw an older couple struggling to get a large, brightly wrapped package into the trunk of a car with Florida plates. I gave them a rope I had in my car and helped the man tie it to his bumper. When the package was secured the man thanked me.

"That's awful nice of you, young man, awful nice."

"You're welcome," I said, and got into my car and headed home.

Comment:

This story begins in **narration**, and deftly uses **indirect quotation** to move the story along: the father's ultimatum in the first paragraph, the imitative "thank you" in the second. The counterman Jerry is a more important character than the boss. Thus, Jerry gets lines of direct dialogue, while the job interview itself is swiftly summarized (but punctuated by the direct quote sarcastic **non-sequitur**, "No shit.").

Jerry's propensity for scatological humor is a nice **limp** to secure his identity in the reader's mind. However, when the story takes a turn toward the serious, Jerry transcends his limp to become a more complex character both to the reader and to the narrator ("This time Jerry was not talking about sex to embarrass me. . . ").

The small scene at the end in which the narrator does a good deed serves as a symbolic **falling action** to bring the story to a fitting close.

POOH

by Diane Moore

WINNIE THE POOH is my bestest friend. Tigger, Eeyore, Piglet, Kanga and Roo are all my friends too. But Pooh is my best friend in the whole world. They all live in the wall in my room. My Daddy's friend painted them there. We all get along real good. We never ever fight or scream. Pooh and I share all our secrets, I know he would never tell anybody my secrets, not a soul. We play tea party, Barbies, and dress up. I have lots of different costumes that my grand-mom made me for Halloween. I like to wear the bride's dress the most, because it is the prettiest.

Pooh wanted to play tea party tonight, but I didn't feel like it. When I told him I didn't want to play he said "Oh, bother." That's what a Pooh bear says when he's disappointed. I've been getting in trouble a lot for not having my homework done. I wish I could just tell my teacher that I can't think right when my Mommy's screaming all the time, but then she would probably think that I was bad. My teacher, Mrs. Daisy, is real nice and I don't want her to think that I'm bad.

I think Mommy is mad because Daddy took me to the Brick Lounge today. I don't understand why this made her so grouchy. I like it when Daddy takes me to the Brick Lounge. I get to sit up in a big stool and drink all the soda I want. Mommy doesn't let me drink soda at home. They have a huge jukebox there and Daddy gives me lots of dimes to put in it. Today I played "Rhinestone Cowboy" two times and "Happy Birthday" three times. I know all the words to "Happy Birthday." There was this big man named Bubba, with a beard like Santa, who I played pool with. Since I can't hold the big stick I get to push the balls with my hand. I won and Bubba gave me a quarter. All my Daddy's friends are real nice. The lady behind the counter said they were getting a video game next week. I hope Daddy will take me back to play.

From The Parts Warehouse: Noteworthy items to look for in this story include: the narrator, closure, and metaphor.

We had to leave when Bubba started

fighting with some other man about the football game on TV. I told Daddy in the car on the way home that I understood, because sometimes the big kids at recess fight when they play football. He just laughed. We stopped at the building with the piles and piles of soda on the way home. Daddy said he needed to get some more beer. I got to get a bag of roasted peanuts.

When we got home, I ran in the house to tell Mommy how much fun I had, but she told me to get to my room. Then she started screaming at Daddy. Maybe she found out Daddy let me drink soda. Mommy is very smart.

I'll watch my TV until it's over. Watching television is the best thing to do when they yell. I sit on the floor real close and turn the volume on real low so Mommy doesn't hear. I'm supposed to be doing my homework. There is a show on about the jungle. Lots of monkeys are swinging in the trees. I wish I could be a monkey.

"Sara! Come here now!"

Uh-oh, better turn off the TV. I run through the living room into the kitchen. Mommy's standing at the door shaking a jar of peanut butter.

"What's the matter, Mommy? Why are you crying?"

"Why, why isn't the lid to the peanut butter jar on correctly?"

"I don't know, Mommy."

"You don't know. YOU DON'T KNOW! When did YOU use the peanut butter last?"

"I don't remember."

"YOU DON'T REMEMBER? I'll ask you one more time. Did you use the peanut butter?"

"I guess so."

"You guess so. Did you put the lid back on correctly?"

"I thought I did."

"Well you thought wrong, Missy."

"I'm sorry Mommy."

"You better start paying attention. Get back to your room, and stay there."

When I walk back to my room, I pass Daddy sitting in his big black chair. He's drinking the beer we got him at the store. He gives me a big smile and wink. I skip back to my room. I hope he doesn't get sick and not be able to go to work again. Then Mommy will be *real* mad. If I said I didn't eat the peanut butter, then she would say I was lying.

Maybe I did eat it and now I just can't remember. I do silly things like that all the time.

I turn the TV on, but the jungle show is over. O, bother. There is some news show on. I don't understand the things they are saying, but it's better than listening to Mommy and Daddy.

After a while, things get spooky quiet and I can hear Daddy fumbling around in the kitchen. He is acting real funny again. I can hear everything Daddy is doing because the sliding doors leading from my room to the kitchen are open a little teeny bit. I hear Daddy getting a glass out. I pray to God with all my heart, "Please don't let him drop it." But God lets him drop it anyway.

As soon as I hear the glass crash against the floor, I jump up and run into the kitchen. I ask Daddy if he is O.K., but he isn't paying attention. He is on the floor petting our puppy Radar. I kneel down to get the dustpan and brush out from under the sink, but it is too late, Mommy is standing in the door, her face is bright, bright red. I want to crawl under the sink, but I can't move.

Mommy is quiet for a long time. Then, in a voice that doesn't sound like my Mommy's, she says, "Sara, pack your clothes." I tip toe back to my room. I hear Daddy start to cry. I want to go back out and give him a big hug and tell him everything is O.K. But everything isn't O.K.

Mommy has gone away when she was mad before, but she has never taken me with her. I wonder how long we will be gone for. Mommy comes in and asks me if I am ready. I put my Holly Hobby coloring book, and my Supergirl UndeRoos in a bag. Mommy takes my backpack and helps me put on my hat and jacket. I hold my yellow blankie in one hand and Pooh holds my other. Together we follow Mommy past Daddy, still crying on the floor, and walk out into the beautiful snowy night.

Pooh and I get in the car and Mommy seat belts us in. Mommy starts the car and pulls out of the driveway. I wave bye-bye to Daddy and Radar and my pretty little house. I really want to ask her where we're going, but she doesn't look very good. I think it's best just to keep quiet. I wish I could reach out and touch the falling snow. The snow is falling real fast. When you look out the window it is real blurry. Too bad I didn't bring my snowsuit. Maybe we're going somewhere where I could play in the snow with Pooh.

The car is hot and stuffy. It makes my mouth dry. I want to roll

down the window, but I'd get in trouble for letting the cold air in.
Pooh is getting heavy on my lap. I ask him to sit in the back seat and
put his seat belt on. I also tell him not to disturb Mommy while she is
driving. She is upset enough already.

Mommy is having a hard time driving. I don't think she can see
where she is going. I ask Mommy if we are going to drive far in the
snow. She says she isn't sure, we will have to pull in somewhere so she
can make a phone call. We drive to the big K-Mart parking lot. All the
lights are shining real bright. Mommy tells me to stay put while she
goes and uses the pay phone.

It is past my bedtime. The heat is making me sleepy. I roll the
window down a little tiny bit, so I can smell the fresh snow. The air
coming in is giving me goose bumps. Pooh doesn't mind having the
window down, because his fur always keeps him warm. Mommy is
taking a long time. The snow looks so beautiful floating around in the
K-Mart parking lot. I wish Pooh and I were home in bed.

I can see Mommy walking back to the car. She looks really cold and
her brown hair is all speckled with white from the snow. She opens the
car door, and sits down. She is shivering a whole lot.

"Roll the GOD DAMN WINDOW UP. IT'S FREEZING, SARA!
ARE YOU CRAZY?"

"No Mommy, I'm not crazy, I like the snow."

I don't know what I said wrong, but Mommy's crying real hard. She
is grabbing me and hugging me real tight. She starts to rock me back
and forth saying my name over and over: "Sara, Sara, Sara," until she
is screaming, "Sara! Sara! Sara!" I just stay real quiet and wait for the
screams to stop. The screams stop, but the crying doesn't. I think
Mommy scared Pooh, because he is curled up in a ball on the floor in
the back. I'm not scared, though. I'm staying brave. I always stay
brave.

Mommy finally lets go of me. She is finished crying. I ask her when
we are going to get going where we are supposed to be going. She
speaks real quiet, and says we won't be able to go anywhere because
the roads are icy and slippery. I ask her if we are going to have to sleep
at the K-Mart. Then she asks me what I think we should do. I tell her
that we should probably go home and put Daddy to bed.

"Then that's what we'll do Sara," she whispers. "Then that's what
we'll do."

On the way home Pooh and I forget to ask Mommy who she was

calling at the K-Mart. I just want to get home and tell Tigger, Piglet, Eeyore, Kanga, and Roo that Pooh and I are safe. I know they must be worried.

When we walk in the door, Daddy is still on the kitchen floor, sleeping with Radar. Mommy wakes him up and tells him to come to bed. We help him walk and tuck him in. I give him a kiss on the cheek. His eyes are all red and puffy and he is mumbling about something. Mommy tells him to hush and rest and asks me to get him a glass of juice. I tip toe out to the kitchen and reach in the cabinet for a glass. Then I remember the glass that Daddy broke. There isn't a mess on the floor anymore. I look in the trash can and find all the broken pieces. What a good Daddy. He remembered to clean up. I pour the juice and bring it back to Mommy and Daddy's room, but Daddy has already fallen asleep. Mommy tells me that I should be asleep too. She says I still may have school tomorrow.

"Go to bed Sara. Sleep tight. I love you."

"I love you too, Mommy."

I go back to my room and take off my jacket and my clothes. Pooh and I laugh at Daddy snoring so loud. I put on my favorite Holly Hobby nightshirt and I turn off the light. When I close my door, I leave it open a tiny bit so the hallway light shines in. I take out my school books and pencil and place them in the light. Then I sit down beside them because I still have homework to do. I'm learning how to add and subtract.

Comment:

To achieve emotional poignancy, a story must avoid **sentimentality**. In presenting this singular sad evening in the life of a dysfunctional family, the author never gives in to the temptation to have her little girl **narrator** beg for the reader's sympathy. Sara is relentlessly straight-forward—she takes each situation in terms of its immediate consequence to her life. When they come home from the Brick Lounge, she fears she will be punished for drinking soda. It is left to the reader to see the bigger picture, to identify this episode as a sample of the father's typical behavior, and to understand the mother's rage and frustration. The author has the courage to risk the reader's sympathy for the mother in the peanut butter scene.

But when mother and daughter are out alone in a discount store parking lot in a blizzard with nowhere to go, the reader is won back by the heart-breaking role reversal that has the mother asking the daughter what they should do.

After all the innocent strength and forgiveness displayed by the narrator, the **closure** is a brilliant choice. The last line employs a simple but unmistakable **metaphor** to convey that none of this will be forgotten, that it all adds up to a powerful impact on her life.

BY THE END OF FEBRUARY

by Alan McCabe

1/20 wed
   something

2/1 fri
   sittin on the dock of the bay watchin my blood drain away wastin
time . . . this sucks

2/4 mon
   write something she says like you used to, remember the one about
the very lonely duck who had to drive a truck (remember like you did
when you were little) I DID write something on wednesday, see?
   don't sleep so much she says gotta keep awake blah blah blah what
the hell else is there to do sitting here six hours a day three days a week
   head hurts so much someone must whack my head in my sleep or
get inside my head and push my eyes out with their thumbs
   SLEEP!!! Sorry diane I can't help it

2/6 wed
   goddamn Mr. Stupidass Walker failing me in algebra, study my ass
off go to class when I can I don't ask for pity but he knows I gotta come
here mon wed fridays he could gimme just a little bit of a break, midterm was
just stupid mistakes anyone could see I know all the stuff.
   not like I can concentrate anyway with Nancy sitting behind me, God
what was she doing to that gum yesterday, I'm sure everyone was looking at
my pants. I came so close to asking her to the prom but christ a guy who looks
like me asking a girl who looks like her that's a joke, shouldn't put her through
the discomfort of having to say no that's gotta be hard for a girl.

> *From*
> *The Parts*
> *Warehouse:*
> *In this story, McCabe*
> *successfully employs*
> *in media res,*
> *exposition,*
> *stream of*
> *consciousness,*
> *and motif.*

hard. christ. get like that here too if my blood and hormones weren't being pumped outa my body

hey good song title, blood and hormones.

2/8 fri

happy anniversary, mike. whoopee.

three years ago today, kidney shuts down they rush me here and give me emergency dialysis. coming here every mon wed friday since. just like old times again, like way back in second grade when the originals shut off. Diane was my nurse back then too. I was her first patient, we're like friends. she has a nice voice, I like when she puts her fingers through my hair. I don't comb my hair, what's left of it.

STORY IDEA: on some other planet some other galaxy they have this war but it's not over money land oil religion, it's about time, cause the one side is always running around with no time for any fun and the other side has nothing but leisure time on their hands. they probably just sleep a lot. yeah that might work.

2/13 wed

mon was such a bad day. tube came undone somehow, blood was spurting all over the dialysis unit whipping all around like when a fireman loses control of his hose. kinda cool in a way. so then I had to get transfused and I threw up plus I was real thirsty. I hate fluid limits.

but I feel better today. better than I have in a while. I go to Doc Graham to ask something and he says like he does, "What the hell do you want, McNee?" but smiling when he says it, and I ask about my hair. he says monoxidyl just might help since I have high blood pressure anyway they could put me on it. Graham's a good guy.

hey! how about this for a band name: Penis Ennui. Tom, my friend, his band needs a name, I suggested that, he thought I said Penis on Wheat.

new patient in the unit today. Di says she's my age though she looks younger like thirteen maybe. that's common we all look younger here. Di says her name's Connie that she normally does the sat tues thursday shift but she switched to this shift temporarily cause she wanted to go to some concert in South Carolina of all places. that's pretty cool. asked Diane what concert, she said some band with a strange name. I said Penis Ennui? She thought I said Pain is All We Eat. that's a good name too.

this Connie is using Frankie's old chair. Frankie died of an infection a month ago the poor bastard. he was the smallest of us all. six years old, I think he looked about three. used to sit real far down in the chair, bundles of blankets even in August. all you saw was this tiny head with huge eyes, his eyes were open all the time. I think he knew he was going to die, and he wanted to take everything in before he kicked. that day was so weird. I got stuck, and there he was right beside me. fell asleep like I usually do, woke up and he was gone. I don't think he ever said three words to me, he was so quiet, but I miss him. one day I felt so mad, cause I passed these interns in the hallway. they were talking about Frankie and they said, "Miracle he lived as long as he did." you don't say that.

still she sleeps. Di says that's not like her but with the trip to Carolina and back and all.

STORY IDEA: some guy loses his penis in the Vietnam war. conflict. young boy, six or so, finds it and brings it back to his starving village. buries it. soon the crops are booming. years later, crops are bad again, and the boy, now like fourteen remembers the penis from the past. can't find any lying around so literally whacks off his own. fellow villagers think he's looney and run him out of town. next month, another great crop.

2/15 fri

Connie is so cool! holy shit! The band she went all the way to South Carolina to see, it was They Might Be Giants! I got to talk to her after treatment on wednes while we waited for our bleeding to stop. I said why didn't you see them here in Philly like I did a month ago and she hit me and said she tried to get tickets but couldn't. besides she has a cousin in Carolina. anyway, we started singing all these TMBG songs and it was just so cool. I told her about that live bootleg of theirs I have and she was so jealous but today I brought the portable CD player and we just listened to it. this is so cool.

she likes to write. she's been published. she saw I have this pen and notebook and I told her how Diane wants me to keep this journal cause I sleep all the time and I should be doing something instead. she asked to see it but I said no it's kinda personal and she said she understood.

she's banging away on this personal word processor she has. working on a novel, she says, and she'll let me read the first draft when she finishes it by the end of february. that's her deadline, she says. I asked isn't this just for yourself, what does a deadline matter? you can finish it whenever you damn well please. she kinda frowned and said you have to have a deadline, otherwise nothing would make you finish. she writes her deadlines in big black letters on posterboard on her bedroom wall then it's like fate, she said, you can't possibly avoid it. it's incredible to watch her as she writes. really gets into it. mouths along as she writes, nods her head when she likes what she writes, bangs on the keyboard and curses when she makes a mistake.

but come on I mean Jesus this is cool! we talked about all the good groups, XTC Pixies Primus Pavement, and everyone! and movies, we had the longest conversation about Eraserhead and then David Lynch. we both started doing the scene where Henry goes to his girlfriend's house for dinner and they have chicken and the blood spurts out and the mom asks have you been having sex with my daughter? man we were in stitches.

then of course we traded hospital horror stories like really bad roommates we've had. I told her about that kid Dickie or Dinkie or whatever the hell his name was who always screamed about roast beef and how he thought the nurses were out to kill him which they very well might have been. and she told me about a roommate of hers who had some kind of farting disease and I just could not top that one.

so we were talking so long today my mouth is dry but fluid limits god damn them. she said we have to stop talking now I've vowed to write two hours a day. writers.

jeez, look at her. typing away like crazy. long thick red hair, green eyes. she has this-oops! caught! my face is red I can feel it. Diane gives me the thumbs up.

2/18 mon

wow, we're just talking up a storm today. first four hours have flown by. she's writing now, because of her writing vow and all. "sorry, Mike," she said, "not even you can keep me from my vow." that's fine by me. I love to watch her. christ what is she writing? can't wait till . . . what, ten days from now, then I get to see it.

HOLY SHIT!! I gotta ask HER to the prom!! I mean, come on, no one at school is this cool! I can't believe I didn't think of this before! we'd have the best time the two of us.

oh man just thinking of it makes my stomach all messed up. how do I do this? can't do it here, we're all so close everyone would hear and go "Aaaaaw!" plus if Connie had to say no that'd make it doubly worse in front of all these people.

what if she did have to say no? that wouldn't be fair to her, and it'd be all uncomfortable in here from now on I mean here we sit eight feet away from each other.

shut up, Mike, you're trying to talk yourself outta this like always. you're gonna do this. you're gonna ask Connie to your senior prom! and you're gonna do it . . . not just yet.

a deadline! I need a deadline! I'll plagiarize hers. February 28th. Mike, you're gonna ask Connie to the prom before the month of February is over. got it? got it. good.

2/22 fri

STORY IDEA: this one's about the scaredest stupid pussy in the whole goddamn world. he's so shit-pants frightened that he hides in his bed all day long life passes him by and he dies. the end.

wednes we talked the whole time. it came time for her to write and she said, "screw it. I'd rather just talk to you." and you just can't understand how good that made me feel I was like up on the ceiling. so then treatment is over and my arm won't stop bleeding. she's sitting out in the waiting room and she sees my arm is getting tired and she holds my arm for me. it's just her and me nobody else around. God damn it! the words were right there, right the hell on my tongue! but I didn't say anything! what am I afraid of? come on, Mike, you sorry piece of . . .

christ. look at her there. eight words. will. you. go. to. the. prom. with. me? I can write 'em. I just can't say 'em.

ding! did you see that lightbulb go on?

2/27 wed

well. Connie's not here. back to her usual shift I guess. wasn't here on Monday either. that's good I was so sick that day, throwin' up, glad she didn't see me like that. still feel terrible. I'm going to sleep. she finishes her rough draft tomorrow.

3/6

God I hate you you sadistic stiff. my life is some kind of series of pathetic jokes to you, right? I cannot see why Mom and Dad believe in you. anything cool in my life that comes along you just take away and I'm left worse off than before. I will never get happy or excited about anything else ever again because I know you'll eventually take it away like you always do. oh a new kidney so I won't have to be on dialysis anymore, screw it just give it to someone else I'll be back on dialysis again eventually. oh hello! your name is Connie? you're the coolest girl I've ever met! I do believe I love you. stay away from me though, you're gonna die, cause God hates me for whatever reason and destroys all my happiness. God, I hate you I hate you I hate you.

3/11 mon
jeez I can't believe I didn't get struck by lightning for writing that on wed. jeez.

Connie died on that Sunday, the day before I was really sick, of some kind of infection. Di didn't even tell me that day, she thought I knew, thought that was why I was sick. can't get Di's face outta my head from the moment when I asked on wed if Connie was back on her old shift. "We thought you knew," she whispered.

this sucks so much. mom, dad, Doc Graham, Di, they've all been trying to talk to me. I mean I appreciate it and all but it's all bullshit. mom tells me this story about her first boyfriend who died, she says she still hasn't gotten over it entirely. thanks a whole helluva lot mom, what's that supposed to do for me?

thought it was bad looking at that empty chair after Frankie died. this. this sucks so much. it's gotta be the damn chair. they oughta burn that thing.

keep playing these conversations in my head I would have –––okay I have to stop now.

3/13 wed
okay now I really don't get things. not only do I not get struck by lightning but I just find out they have a kidney for me. good grief, I don't know how to feel.

this could very well be my last dialysis Di tells me, what with all the great new drugs they have. I don't know I just can't feel . . . anything.

oh well, my friends will visit me in the hospital probably that'll be nice. breakfast in bed. maybe I'll get some presents.

Comment:

The diary form of this story plunges the reader *in medias res*, showing us the reason for the journal, its halting beginnings, and the world out of which it is written all at the same time. First the writer roots us firmly in the reality of the moment, and then, in the fifth entry, provides **exposition** to let us know the background of the narrator's situation. The run-on sentences and haphazard capitalization create a **stream of consciousness** effect—it seems as if the narrator is transcribing his thoughts as they occur to him.

The rising action of this story is built upon a deadline **motif**. Connie's deadline to finish her novel becomes the narrator's deadline to ask her to the prom, and both prove futile as a terrible literalness overtakes the word: her line is dead. At the climax, the narrator's wretched, God-cursing despair is mitigated, even made ironic, by the fact that the narrator suddenly has the kidney available that he presumably has been waiting for—a good use of *deus ex machina*.

HOLLOW

by Heather Mead

IWOKE UP this morning to the sound of a bird flying into the window. I lay there for a while until I realized no one else was in the house, then got up. Pulled a sweater on over my nightshirt and headed for the deck. I watched the mist hover in the air over the pond, until the sun broke through. I lit my first cigarette of the day and contemplated getting dressed. I decided against it. I'm never sure where to put the ashes and butts because he can't find out that I've started smoking. Usually, I put them in a coffee mug until it's full, and then bury the remains in the flower garden. I don't think he knows.

Sami is feasting on the remains of the bird that woke me up, his tail flicking back and forth with contentment. Benny is lying on his back, his legs fully extended, paws digging at the air. At this moment, the only thing I want is to spend forever here in my rocking chair, smoke, and pretend that I live in a world where he does not exist.

So I sit here some more and wonder why I have stayed so long. I have been with Joe since the day he drove into the gas station where I work. I filled his tank with premium, he paid with cash, and asked when I got off work. Midnight. He'd be back. Two hours later, I locked the safe, climbed in his Ford pick-up, and we headed for Ned's Tavern. We played pool and darts and drank Moosehead. There was something good about being with him; it worried me. I kept waiting for the other shoe to drop. Three years later, I still am.

> *From The Parts Warehouse: Skillful underwriting, and the use of mood and minimalism are features which make this story succeed.*

Sami's tail stops flicking and Benny's starts wagging. Coming up the long, dirt driveway is Joe in his blue pick-up, kicking up dust behind. As usual, my stomach drops somewhere around my knees. With a final exhale, I put the remains in the mug and go inside to hide it in my closet. I crouch in the doorway and wait until I hear the door open then close. He's home.

I walk into the kitchen, buttoning the

fly of my jeans, then sit at the counter to pull on my boots. They are tied before he says anything.

"Mornin'."

"Hey." I am pouring him a glass of grape juice.

"Up long?"

"Nah, half an hour."

"Hm. Got the washer for this sink. I'll work on it this afternoon."

"Whenever." I can't possibly love him.

"So. You going to the store today?"

"Do I need to?"

He is standing behind me, one hand on my waist, the other playing with my hair. "Well, I thought maybe we could eat home tonight. But there's nothing to cook. And I'm out of beer."

I turn to look at him, thereby pulling my hair out of his hands. I'm okay as long as he isn't touching me. His eyes are so brown, so huge that I forget to breathe if I look directly into them. I watch as he casually tucks his long hair behind an ear, and remember why I jumped into his truck without a first thought. "Yeah, well we need some other things too. I guess I'll head out now."

He cups my chin in his hands and pulls me toward him. Shit.

"You okay?"

No. "Yeah. I'm just not awake yet. Give me an hour or three."

His eyes catch mine and won't let go. It's like he's trying to see into my brain. It won't work. Using every ounce of strength I don't have, I close my eyes and break the spell. Then I am able to turn away.

"Ya need anything else?" I grab my bag and keys, clutch the knob, and hold my breath, waiting for escape.

"Elly." That's it.

"I'll grab some chicken or maybe steaks if they're nice. We can throw them on the grill. I'll make a salad. Maybe I'll get some wine. Red. Okay? See ya."

What am I saying? It doesn't matter, I just need to get out of here. There is a tightness in my chest. I am suffocating. At the car, I look back and Joe is standing in the doorway, arms crossed, hair hanging over his left eye. "Hose the deck down, Sami got another bird."

I start the car, put in a tape, and accelerate down the driveway. At the bottom, I stop to light a cigarette. In the rearview mirror I can see Joe unwinding the hose to clean the deck. Feeling like shit, I turn right out of the driveway and head south on Clover Street.

The first night we spent together, Joe said that he thought it was cool—my working at a gas station. To me it was just money. Since then, it's gotten clearer that we don't look at things the same way. He can't understand why I sit on the deck for hours at a time, not saying or doing anything. I don't understand how he can wake up every morning at six o'clock.

I pull into the shopping center and park an equal distance between the grocery and liquor stores. I buy steak, red wine, and vodka. I flirt with a stockboy in the grocery and the cashier in the liquor store. Later, I drive through the new development and wonder what is going on in the houses, create scenarios, unsure if I could live that kind of life.

Tomorrow is Mom's birthday and I wonder if I should call her. I haven't talked to her since Christmas, and haven't seen her since I left home six years ago and moved here. One small town to another, nothing changes but the street names.

Today I wake up to silence and a cold bed. Joe leaves for work at seven thirty. His crew usually starts at eight. They are finishing a roof today, so he'll probably be late. I lie naked beneath a quilt Joe's grandma made for us when we moved in together. Sami jumps on the bed as I flip my pillow to the cool side. I have two hours before I go to work, and nothing to do. Sami curls up on Joe's pillow and goes to sleep. Benny is pawing at the side door. With a grunt, I get out of bed, throw on Joe's t-shirt, and head for the kitchen.

From the porch, I can see Mrs. Wheeler hanging her blue striped bed sheets. There is a sinking sensation in my stomach. I know this is my life. Twenty years from now, I will still be sitting on this chair, on this porch. Only then it will be my blue striped sheets on the line and my children's overalls hanging in descending order.

It is the same feeling I had two months ago; those three days in April I thought I was pregnant. Seventy-two hours from calling the doctor until the negative result came back. My joy of relief was interrupted by Joe's quiet disappointment. I hadn't told him until I was sure it was a no. All he said was "Oh." He hardly spoke until I gave in and asked what was wrong.

"Would it have been that terrible if you were pregnant?" Pause. "I mean would having my baby be so awful?"

"No Joe, not just your baby, but any baby."

"Why?"

"I'm twenty-three, Joe. I work at a gas station. I barely finished high school. I have no clue what I'm doing, and no idea where I'm heading. Not the best time to have a kid."

He took a step towards me, pulled me into his arms, and said with sincerity. "I'd take care of you, Elly. I'll always take care of you."

What could I possibly say to make him understand that the thought of loving him cannot exist? Without hurting him. God, I didn't want to hurt him.

So I didn't say anything. I accepted his arms, his mouth, and returned them with my own. Sometimes when it's dark out, and quiet, just him and me, I believe it could work. But then the sun comes up.

I extinguish my cigarette, collect the remains, and head for the shower.

When I get home from work, Joe is sitting on the porch, drinking a beer and playing with Benny. A jolt flashes through my body. Without looking, he passes me a half-empty bottle of red wine. My favorite.

"Thanks, hon. How's the roof going?"

"When did you start smoking?"

Damn.

"A few months ago."

"Were you planning to tell me?"

"I wasn't aware I had to report back to you."

"I wasn't asking for a report. I just wondered if you were going to tell me."

Good question. I don't know. I drink from the bottle and look out at the lightning bugs. Benny is rolling on his back so Joe can scratch his stomach. There is a new can of beer in Joe's hand and three empties lying at his feet. He has not looked at me.

"I guess I'm just wondering why you never tell me anything. Not until it's already over and done with."

"Well I know you don't like the smell of cigarettes, so I figured . . ."

"I'm not talking about the damn cigarettes."

"Then what . . . "

"*Hey Joe, good news. I thought I was pregnant but I'm not. Oh by the way, did I mention my father shot himself?* Christ, Elly, you went to the funeral without me."

"I didn't go."

"What?"

"I didn't go."

"But you went home."

"No, I went to Norfolk. I planned to go home, but I couldn't."

Joe has moved to the railing, and rests his hands on the top bar. Benny keeps pawing at his ankle but Joe is not aware. I sit on the third step and lean back against the landing. I close my eyes and exhale slowly. This is it. After three years, the second shoe is dropping.

"Why didn't you tell me?"

"I didn't have anything to say."

"You never have anything to say. Not anymore. Not to me."

I have no clue how to respond to him, because everything he is saying is true. I lay my head against the landing. If I can block him out, pretend I'm talking to myself, maybe I can get through this. "When my dad . . . died . . . I knew it didn't matter if someone else could make you happy, you had to make yourself happy. Depending on someone else is just setting yourself up, and when they screw you over, you're left with nothing."

Joe still has not looked at me. I don't know if he is there or if he has left. It doesn't matter. I can't stop now. "I don't want this anymore."

He lifts his head, as if to look at the stars, but I know that his eyes are closed. He opens his mouth, pauses then speaks.

"Don't want what?" There is hollowness in his voice.

"I don't want . . . to be here anymore. I want to go somewhere I've never been before, somewhere I know nothing about." He can't make me say it.

"And you don't want me to go with you." It is not a question.

"Everything is here for you, your job, friends, family. You can't leave it all." It's the truth.

"And you can't stay."

"No."

Neither of us has moved in the last five minutes. All I can see is an outline and his hair, softer than mine will ever be, and for once I am not jealous.

I stand up and walk into the house. In the bedroom, I pack my things. There is little and I'm done in thirty minutes. As a last thought, I grab his red shirt and throw it in a box. I carry my things out the side door and load my car. My life in two bags, two boxes and a backpack.

"I better be going." But I don't move.

Then he is turning to me, holding me to him and kissing me. I respond, feeling what I've always felt when he kissed me. He releases me. I back away and look up into his eyes, the ones that make me forget to breathe. I know this should be the big moment, the one where I confess everything to him and end up staying. Nothing happens. I feel no need to tell him anything. He knows this and watches as I walk back down the steps and to my car. I pause at the door for a moment, wondering if there is any way. . . no, none. I get behind the wheel, turn the key, flip on the lights, and slowly start down the driveway. About halfway, I lightly touch the brake. In the rearview mirror, Joe is just a shadow—an outline, yet I think at that moment he is more than I will ever be. I tap the gas pedal and continue my descent. At the end, I turn right and head into the darkness.

Comment:

This story won the Fiction Prize in the winter 1994 issue of *The Lantern,* the literary magazine of Ursinus College. The judge, Dr. Patricia Schroeder, eloquently explains her choice:

I chose "Hollow" for its unity of effect. Although we never know the exact source of the narrator's emotional emptiness, her hollowness of spirit emerges on every level of the story. The effect is palpable in the non-event that marks the crisis in the plot, in dialogue that conceals rather than reveals, and in the specific, concrete objects. Every word, every image, conveys the interior hollowness that the narrator laments but cannot undo, and that the author of the story conveys with convincing emotional truth.

Index